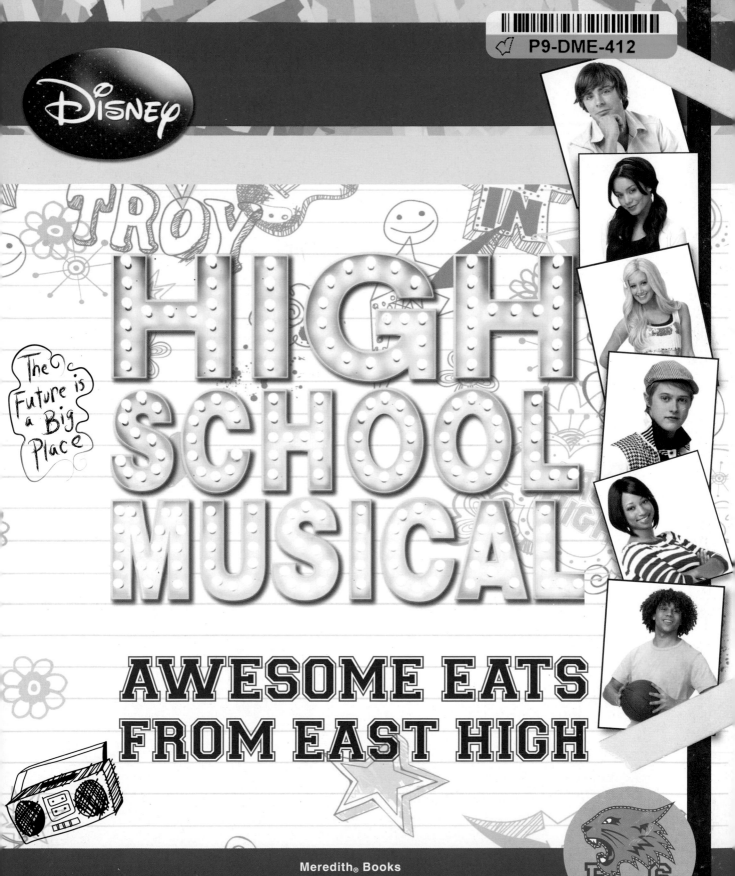

P9-DME-412

DISNEY

The Future is a Big Place

TROY HIGH SCHOOL MUSICAL

AWESOME EATS FROM EAST HIGH

Meredith® Books
Des Moines, Iowa

EHS

WILDCATS

Based on the Disney Channel Original Movie
"High School Musical," Written by Peter Barsocchini
Based on "High School Musical 2," Written by Peter Barsocchini
Based on Characters Created by Peter Barsocchini.

Based on "High School Musical 3," Based on the screenplay written by Peter Barsocchini
Based on characters created by Peter Barsocchini
Executive Producer Kenny Ortega
Produced by Bill Borden and Barry Rosenbush
Directed by Kenny Ortega

Copyright © 2008 by Disney Enterprises, Inc.

All rights reserved. No part of this book
may be reproduced in any form without
written permission from the publisher.

Meredith®
BOOKS

Meredith Books
1716 Locust Street
Des Moines, IA 50309-3023
meredithbooks.com

Printed in China.
First Edition.
ISBN: 978-0-696-24000-3

Editor: Sheena Chihak, R.D.
Art Direction: Chad Jewell
Graphic Design and Support Illustration: Mada Design, Inc.

TABLE OF CONTENTS DiVE IN

WILDCATS

GETTING STARTED

HEY, WILDCAT!

JOIN THE KIDS FROM **EAST HIGH** AS THEY TAKE THE FLOOR—THE KITCHEN FLOOR—TO WHIP UP SOME **AWESOME EATS!**

Soon you'll be chowing down on Bolton Burgers, Sharpastries, and Wildcat Red & White Bites. You can make many of these recipes by yourself, but it's best to have an adult nearby to help out, especially when you're working with appliances and utensils that could burn or cut you. Once you get the hang of chopping, measuring, mixing, and mashing, the kitchen will be your stage and you will be the star. You can "Bet On It."

4

YOUR RECIPE FOR SUCCESS

Preparing the perfect recipe is easy! The steps in a recipe are just like parts of a musical performance—the warm-up, waiting in the wings, during the show, and the encore.

The Warm-Up

- Read the entire recipe from beginning to end with an adult. Ask yourself: Do I know exactly what I'm supposed to do? If there's anything you don't understand, ask the adult for help.

- If you have any food allergies or intolerances, read the ingredients carefully to be sure all the foods are safe for you to eat.

- Check your ingredients. Make sure you have enough of all the required ingredients. If you don't, make a list of the things you need and ask an adult to help you get them.

- Check your utensils. Gather all the utensils and equipment you'll need to prepare the recipe. If you're missing anything, ask an adult for help.

Waiting in the Wings

- Wash fresh fruits and veggies in cool water before eating or preparing them.

- Never use cracked or dirty eggs.

- Always wash your hands with soap and water for at least 20 seconds before you begin cooking.

During the Show

- Measure ingredients accurately.

- Follow the recipe step-by-step. Finish each step in the recipe before starting the next. Don't take shortcuts.

- Use good food safety habits. Cook and eat only fresh foods. After working with eggs, raw poultry, seafood, or meat, wash your hands, equipment, and work surfaces, including cutting boards and countertops.

- Be safe. Do not use knives or other sharp equipment without an adult's permission and supervision.

The Encore

- Put leftovers away as soon as possible. Leftovers should never sit out for more than 2 hours.

- Put away all ingredients and equipment.

- Clean up. Throw away trash such as food wrappers and empty packages. Load dirty dishes in the dishwasher or wash and dry them. Wipe counters and table with hot, soapy water.

WILDCATS

WILDCATS

AWESOME EATS FROM EAST HIGH

OPENING NIGHT RECIPES

PLAY THE LEAD
with these showstopping recipes that are sure to earn you a standing ovation. No need to worry about opening night jitters because you choose who gets front-row seats at the dinner table.

ACT 1
Director's Choice Breakfast Bowls
Sharpastries

PLAYING THE LEAD
Crowd-Pleasing Pizza   Perfectly Composed Pizza So
Bolton Burgers   Top-Billing Taco Salad

SUPPORTING ROLES
Front-Row Fruit Salads
Co-President Potatoes

FINAL ACT
Chad's Nutty Apple Crisp
Zeke's Perfect Crème Brûlée

AWESOME EATS FROM EAST HIGH

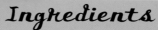

BERRY-SWIRLED OATMEAL

1. If you are using frozen raspberries or strawberries, thaw them following the directions on the package.

2. Put fresh or thawed raspberries or strawberries and honey in a medium bowl. Use potato masher to mash berries or use a wooden spoon to slightly crush the berries. Stir with wooden spoon to mix well. Save for Step 4.

3. Put the water and oats in a medium saucepan and stir with wooden spoon to mix. Put the saucepan on a burner. Turn the burner to medium-high heat. Cook just until bubbly, stirring all the time with wooden spoon. Turn off burner. Use hot pads to remove saucepan from heat. Place saucepan on cooling rack. Cover saucepan with lid. Let oatmeal stand 5 minutes.

4. Spoon the oatmeal into the cereal bowls. Use a clean spoon to spoon raspberry or strawberry mixture over oatmeal in bowls. Gently swirl berries into the oatmeal. If you like, top with additional chopped berries. Makes 4 servings.

Nutrition Facts per serving: 148 calories, 4 g total fat, 3 mg cholesterol, 106 mg sodium, 25 g carbohydrate, 5 g fiber, 3 g protein.

Ingredients

2 cups fresh raspberries or frozen lightly sweetened red raspberries or unsweetened whole strawberries

2 tablespoons honey

3 cups water

1½ cups quick-cooking rolled oats

Fresh raspberries or strawberries, chopped, if you like

Utensils

Measuring cups
Measuring spoons
Medium bowl
Potato masher, if you like
Wooden spoon
Medium saucepan with lid
Hot pads
Cooling rack
Large spoons
4 cereal bowls

ACT I

DIRECTOR'S CHOICE BREAKFAST BOWLS

You've got to be focused and alert for class with Ms. Darbus or you could wind up in detention. Refuel with one of these warm cereal bowls and you'll have her saying, "Brava!"

PEANUT BUTTER BANANA OATMEAL

1. Peel banana. On cutting board, use table knife to slice banana. Save for Step 3.

2. Put the water, apple juice, and oats in a medium saucepan. Stir with a wooden spoon to mix. Put saucepan on a burner. Turn on burner to medium heat. Cook just until bubbly, stirring all the time with a wooden spoon. Turn off burner. Use hot pads to remove saucepan from burner. Place saucepan on cooling rack. Cover saucepan with lid. Let oatmeal stand 5 minutes. Add peanut butter and stir with wooden spoon until combined.

3. Spoon into cereal bowls. Top with banana slices. If you like, sprinkle with miniature semisweet chocolate pieces. Makes 4 servings.

Nutrition Facts per serving: 275 calories, 10 g total fat, 0 mg cholesterol, 80 mg sodium, 41 g carbohydrate, 5 g fiber, 9 g protein.

Ingredients

- 1 banana
- 1½ cups water
- 1½ cups apple juice
- 1½ cups quick-cooking rolled oats
- ¼ cup peanut butter
- 1 tablespoon miniature semisweet chocolate pieces, if you like

Utensils

Measuring cups
Measuring spoons
Cutting board
Table knife
Medium saucepan with lid
Wooden spoon
Hot pads
Cooling rack
4 cereal bowls

FOOD FACT

About 200 million pounds of honey are produced in America every year! Each American eats about 1.29 pounds of this honey each year.

Queen of Lava Springs

Sharpay

SHARPASTRIES

What better way to start your day than with Sharpay's favorite food—pastries! These peach-packed turnovers are easy to make and sure to please, even without imported ingredients.

1. Turn on oven to 400°F. Line a baking sheet with foil; coat foil with nonstick cooking spray. Save for Step 3. Open the package of cinnamon rolls. Separate dough into rounds. Use the palm of your hand to flatten each round into a 4½-inch circle. Save for Step 2.

2. Put peach preserves and cinnamon in a small bowl. Stir with a wooden spoon to mix well. Use table knife to spread preserves mixture over each dough circle to within ¾ inch of edge. Place one or two peach slices on each dough round. (If necessary, use a sharp knife to cut peach slices to fit.) Use a pastry brush to brush dough edges lightly with water. Fold dough over to enclose peach slices. Using the tines of a fork, press around the open edge to seal each turnover. Prick top of each turnover with the fork.

3. Place turnovers on prepared baking sheet. Bake about 12 minutes or until golden brown. Turn off oven. Use hot pads to remove baking sheet from oven. Use a pancake turner to move turnovers to a cooling rack. If you like, drizzle turnovers with icing from package. Cool slightly; serve warm. Makes 8 pastries.

Nutrition Facts per pastry: 151 calories, 2 g total fat, 0 mg cholesterol, 327 mg sodium, 31 g carbohydrate, 1 g fiber, 2 g protein.

Ingredients

Nonstick cooking spray
1   12-ounce package refrigerated reduced-fat cinnamon rolls
⅓   cup low-sugar peach preserves or apricot preserves
⅛   teaspoon ground cinnamon or ground nutmeg
1   15-ounce can peach slices in light syrup, drained

Utensils

Measuring cups
Measuring spoons
Large baking sheet
Foil
Ruler
Small bowl
Wooden spoon
Table knife
Can opener
Colander
Sharp knife, if you like
Pastry brush
Fork
Hot pads
Pancake turner
Cooling rack

QUEEN of Lava Springs

BACKSTAGE PASS Sharpay tries to eliminate her competition for the lead in the musical by persuading Ms. Darbus to hold callbacks at the same time as the scholastic decathlon and the championship basketball game so Troy and Gabriella can't audition.

WILDCATS

EAST HIGH Presents

STAR Dazzle

PLAYING THE LEAD

CROWD-PLEASING PIZZA

Performances by Gabriella always get the crowd on their feet.
Serve this meal and your dinner guests will call for an encore.

1. Turn on oven to 450°F. Put bread shell on a large baking sheet. Place baking sheet in oven. Bake 5 minutes. Use hot pads to remove baking sheet from oven and place on cooling rack.

2. Meanwhile, on cutting board, use sharp knife to cut green pepper in half from top to bottom. Pull off the stem and throw away. Remove seeds and soft white parts from inside pepper halves and throw away. Cut pepper into thin strips. Save for Step 3.

3. Using a rubber scraper, spread pizza sauce evenly on the bread shell. Top with pepperoni, green pepper, red onion, and drained pineapple. Sprinkle with mozzarella cheese.

4. Put baking sheet in oven. Bake 10 to 12 minutes or until cheese is melted and pizza is heated through. Turn off oven. Use hot pads to remove baking sheet from oven. Place baking sheet on cooling rack. Use a pizza cutter to cut pizza into wedges. Makes 4 to 6 servings.

Nutrition Facts per serving: 219 calories, 6 g total fat, 18 mg cholesterol, 509 mg sodium, 32 g carbohydrate, 4 g fiber, 12 g protein.

Ingredients

- 1   12-inch whole wheat thin Italian bread shell (such as Boboli® brand)
- 1   small green sweet pepper
- ½   cup pizza sauce
- ½   cup sliced turkey pepperoni (about 1½ ounces)
- ½   cup thinly sliced quartered red onion
- 1   8-ounce can pineapple slices (juice pack)
- ¾   cup shredded part-skim mozzarella cheese (3 ounces)

Utensils

Measuring cups
Large baking sheet
Hot pads
Cooling rack
Cutting board
Sharp knife
Rubber scraper
Can opener
Colander
Pizza cutter

Dive in!

Gabriella

EAST HIGH

Star Dazzle

We're in This Together

WORK IT OUT

Spending too many hours sitting in front of the TV can turn you into a couch potato. Instead get on your feet and put on your own show for family and friends.

Ingredients

12 ounces lean ground beef

Salt

Black pepper

4 slices favorite reduced-fat cheese, if you like

4 whole wheat or whole grain hamburger buns (buy split buns)

Toppings you like (such as ketchup, mustard, barbecue sauce, mayonnaise, lettuce leaves, tomato slices, purchased salsa, and/or dill or sweet pickle slices)

Utensils

Waxed paper
Ruler
12-inch skillet
Pancake turner
Instant-read thermometer
Hot pads
Cooling rack
Serving plate

TROY

PLAYING THE LEAD

BOLTON BURGERS

DIVE IN

From captain on the court to captain in the kitchen, Troy's specialty
is this basic burger topped any way you like it!

1. Place a piece of waxed paper on the counter or table. Put the ground beef on the waxed paper. Use your hands to divide the meat into four equal portions. Shape each portion into a flat, round patty that measures about 3½ inches across.

2. Put ground beef patties in a skillet. Put skillet on a burner. Turn the burner to medium heat. Cook about 6 minutes or until patties are browned on the bottom. To check, lift patties with the pancake turner and peek underneath.

3. Use the pancake turner to turn over each patty. Sprinkle patties with salt and pepper. Cook 4 to 6 minutes more or until patties are done (160°F).* Top each patty with one slice of the cheese, if you like. Cook about 1 minute more or until cheese begins to melt. Turn off burner. Use hot pads to remove skillet from burner. Place skillet on cooling rack.

4. Place bottom halves of the hamburger buns on a serving plate. Use the pancake turner to place a patty on each bun bottom. Add the toppings you like. Cover with bun tops. Makes 4 servings.

Nutrition Facts per serving: 298 calories, 11 g total fat, 58 mg cholesterol, 569 mg sodium, 21 g carbohydrate, 2 g fiber, 27 g protein.

Indoor Grill Directions: Turn on an indoor grill and adjust the heat to medium if you can. Let grill heat for 10 minutes or for the time given in manufacturer's directions. Carefully place ground beef patties on grill rack. If using a grill with a cover, close the lid. Grill for 5 to 6 minutes or until patties are done (160°F).* If using a grill without a cover, grill patties for 6 minutes; turn patties over using a pancake turner. Grill for 6 to 8 minutes more or until patties are done (160°F).*

*Note: It is very important to cook ground beef patties completely. Do not check the doneness by looking at the color of the meat. Instead ask an adult to help you check the temperature with an instant-read thermometer. Patties are done when the centers reach 160°F.

EAST HIGH
TROY

BACKSTAGE PASS When wishing the drama club good luck, Troy wears the exclamation point to spell the message "Go Drama Club!"

PLAYING THE LEAD

PERFECTLY COMPOSED PIZZA SOUP

Kelsi spends a lot of time at the piano composing perfect music, but it won't take you long to create this soup masterpiece.

1. On cutting board, use sharp knife to thinly slice sausage. Save for Step 3.

2. Put onion, green pepper, mushrooms, zucchini, and ¼ cup of the beef broth in a medium saucepan. Put saucepan on burner. Turn burner to medium-high heat. Bring to boiling; reduce heat to medium. Cover saucepan with lid and simmer for 5 minutes, stirring now and then with the wooden spoon.

3. Use the wooden spoon to stir in the remaining broth, the undrained tomatoes, the tomato sauce, sausage, and pizza seasoning. Turn burner to medium-high. Bring to boiling; reduce heat to medium. Simmer 5 to 10 minutes more or until vegetables are tender, stirring now and then with wooden spoon. Turn off burner. Use hot pads to remove saucepan from heat. Place saucepan on cooling rack.

4. Ladle soup into soup bowls. Top with mozzarella cheese. Makes 6 servings.

Nutrition Facts per serving: 114 calories, 3 g total fat, 18 mg cholesterol, 696 mg sodium, 14 g carbohydrate, 2 g fiber, 7 g protein.

Ingredients

4   ounces cooked smoked turkey sausage
1   cup chopped onion
1   cup chopped green sweet pepper
1   cup sliced fresh mushrooms
1   cup sliced halved zucchini
1   14-ounce can reduced-sodium beef broth
1   14½-ounce can diced tomatoes with basil, garlic, and oregano, undrained
1   8-ounce can no-salt-added tomato sauce
½   teaspoon pizza seasoning
½   cup shredded reduced-fat mozzarella cheese (2 ounces)

Utensils

Measuring cups
Measuring spoons
Cutting board
Sharp knife
Medium saucepan with lid
Wooden spoon
Can opener
Hot pads
Cooling rack
Ladle
6 soup bowls

FOOD FACT

Most grocery stores sell red, white, and yellow onions. All onions, no matter what color, contain substances called sulfuric compounds that can make your eyes water. Don't let watery eyes stop you from eating them. The vitamin C and fiber in onions are good for you.

Ingredients

4	6- to 8-inch whole wheat or plain flour tortillas
	Nonstick cooking spray
1	medium onion
12	cherry tomatoes
12	ounces lean ground beef or uncooked ground turkey
½	teaspoon bottled minced garlic
1	8-ounce can tomato sauce
1	tablespoon vinegar
½	teaspoon ground cumin
¼	teaspoon crushed red pepper
4	cups shredded lettuce
¼	cup shredded reduced-fat cheddar cheese (1 ounce)
¼	cup chopped green or red sweet pepper, if you like

Utensils

Measuring cups	Cutting board
Measuring spoons	Sharp knife
Foil	Large skillet
Four 10-ounce custard cups	Wooden spoon
Hot pads	Colander
Cooling rack	Medium bowl
Baking sheet	Disposable container

PLAYING THE LEAD

TOP-BILLING TACO SALAD

Gabriella's fantastic audition lands her the lead role in the school musical.
With this amazing meal, you're sure to be the star of the kitchen!

1. Turn on oven to 350°F. Wrap tortillas in a sheet of foil. Bake 10 minutes. While tortillas bake, coat four 10-ounce custard cups with nonstick spray. Use hot pads to remove tortillas from oven and place on cooling rack. Unwrap tortillas. Carefully press one tortilla into each custard cup. Place custard cups on a baking sheet. Place baking sheet in oven. Bake 10 to 15 minutes or until tortillas are golden brown and crisp. Turn off oven. Use hot pads to remove baking sheet from oven and place on cooling rack. Let cool completely. When tortilla cups are cool, carefully remove from custard cups. Save for Step 5.*

2. While tortillas bake, on cutting board, use sharp knife to cut onion into small pieces. Save for Step 3. Use sharp knife to cut cherry tomatoes into fourths. Save for Step 5.

3. Put ground beef, onion, and garlic into a large skillet. Put skillet on a burner. Turn burner to medium-high heat. Break up meat with a wooden spoon. Cook until no pink color is left in the meat, stirring now and then with the wooden spoon. This will take about 10 minutes. Turn off burner. Use hot pads to remove skillet from burner and place on cooling rack. Place colander over a medium bowl. Spoon meat mixture and juices into the colander and let the juices drain into the bowl. Spoon meat back into skillet. Put cooled juices in a disposable container and throw away.

4. Stir tomato sauce, vinegar, cumin, and red pepper into meat mixture. Use hot pads to return skillet to burner. Turn burner to medium-high heat. Bring to boiling; reduce heat to medium. Simmer, uncovered, 10 minutes, stirring now and then with wooden spoon. Turn off burner. Use hot pads to remove skillet from burner. Place skillet on cooling rack.

5. Place a tortilla cup on each plate. Spoon meat mixture into tortilla cups. Sprinkle with the lettuce, cheese, and, if you like, sweet pepper. Top with the tomatoes. Makes 4 servings.

*Note: You can make the tortilla bowls up to 1 month before you need them. Place the cooled bowls in a large freezer container with paper towels between bowls. Also crumple paper towels around the sides of the container to protect the bowls. Seal, label, and freeze up to 1 month.

Nutrition Facts per serving: 297 calories, 13 g total fat, 59 mg cholesterol, 575 mg sodium, 23 g carbohydrate, 3 g fiber, 22 g protein.

Dive in!

BACKSTAGE **PASS** Gabriella plays the lead role of Minnie in East High's winter musical, *Twinkle Towne*. Sharpay is her understudy.

FRUIT DUET SALAD

1. Turn on oven to 350°F. Put almonds in pie pan. Place pie pan in oven. Bake 5 minutes. Use hot pads to remove pie pan from oven. Use wooden spoon to stir almonds. Use hot pads to return pie pan to oven. Bake about 5 minutes more or until almonds are a light golden brown. Turn off oven. Use hot pads to remove pie pan from oven and place on cooling rack. Save for Step 3.

2. For dressing, put vinegar, orange juice, oil, sugar, and dry mustard in a small screw-top jar. Screw lid onto jar and shake well.

3. Place salad greens in a large salad bowl. Pour dressing over greens. Toss gently to coat. Put orange sections and raspberries on top of greens. Sprinkle with almonds. Makes 6 (1-cup) servings.

Nutrition Facts per serving: 89 calories, 5 g total fat, 0 mg cholesterol, 10 mg sodium, 10 g carbohydrate, 2 g fiber, 2 g protein.

Ingredients

- ¼ cup sliced almonds
- 1 tablespoon red wine vinegar
- 1 tablespoon orange juice
- 1 tablespoon olive oil or canola oil
- 1 teaspoon sugar
- ¼ teaspoon dry mustard
- 6 cups torn mixed salad greens (such as baby spinach, Bibb lettuce, and/or escarole)
- 1 10½-ounce can mandarin orange sections (juice pack), drained
- ½ cup fresh raspberries

Utensils

Measuring cups
Measuring spoons
Pie pan
Hot pads
Wooden spoon
Cooling rack
Can opener
Colander
Small screw-top jar with lid
Large salad bowl

FRONT-ROW FRUIT SALADS

Serve these sweet sides and a chair at your dinner table will be the best seat in the house.

STAR-STUDDED SALAD

1. Place cantaloupe and honeydew melon in a medium bowl. Drizzle honey and lime juice over melon. Use a wooden spoon to gently toss to mix. Cover with plastic wrap and chill in the refrigerator up to 24 hours.

2. To serve, add mint and toss gently with a wooden spoon to mix. Sprinkle with fresh berries. Makes 4 to 6 servings.

Nutrition Facts per serving: 96 calories, 0 g total fat, 0 mg cholesterol, 29 mg sodium, 24 g carbohydrate, 2 g fiber, 1 g protein.

Ingredients

2   cups chilled cantaloupe cut into 1-inch star shapes, cubes, or balls

2   cups chilled honeydew melon cut into 1-inch star shapes, cubes, or balls

1   tablespoon honey

1   teaspoon lime juice

1   tablespoon snipped fresh mint

1   cup fresh blueberries and/or red raspberries

Utensils

Measuring cups
Measuring spoons
Tiny star-shaped cutter or melon baller
Sharp knife
Kitchen scissors
Medium bowl
Wooden spoon
Plastic wrap

Get'cha HEAD in the GAME

FOOD FACT Berries such as raspberries and blueberries contain a lot of vitamin C, which keeps your teeth and bones strong and even helps protect you from infections.

RYAN

SUPPORTING ROLES

CO-PRESIDENT POTATOES

As co-president of the drama club, Ryan knows supporting roles, like choreographer, are important to putting on a great show. Serve this side dish with a fantastic entrée to put together the perfect meal.

1. Let potatoes stand at room temperature to thaw or place a colander in sink, put potatoes in colander, and rinse with cold water to thaw. Turn on oven to 350°F. Lightly coat a 2-quart rectangular baking dish with nonstick cooking spray. Save for Step 3.

2. Pour soup into a very large bowl. Add cheddar cheese, milk, sour cream, onion, pepper, and salt. Add potatoes and stir with a wooden spoon to mix.

3. Spoon potato mixture into prepared baking dish, spreading evenly with the wooden spoon. Cover with foil. Place baking dish in oven. Bake 45 minutes. Use hot pads to carefully pull out oven rack. Use wooden spoon to stir potatoes. Sprinkle mixture with cornflakes. Use hot pads to carefully push oven rack back in place.

4. Bake, uncovered, 20 to 25 minutes more or until heated through and bubbly. Turn off oven. Use hot pads to remove baking dish from oven and place on cooling rack. Let stand 10 minutes. Makes 12 servings.

Nutrition Facts per serving: 129 calories, 3 g total fat, 11 mg cholesterol, 236 mg sodium, 20 g carbohydrate, 1 g fiber, 5 g protein.

Ingredients

1   30- or 32-ounce package frozen shredded or diced hash brown potatoes
    Nonstick cooking spray
1   10¾-ounce can reduced-fat and reduced-sodium condensed cream of chicken soup
1   cup shredded reduced-fat sharp cheddar cheese (4 ounces)
¾   cup fat-free milk
½   cup light dairy sour cream
⅓   cup finely chopped onion or 2 tablespoons dried minced onion
½   teaspoon black pepper
¼   teaspoon salt
½   cup crushed cornflakes or crushed wheat cereal flakes

Utensils

Measuring cups
Measuring spoons
Colander, if you like
2-quart rectangular baking dish
Can opener
Very large bowl
Wooden spoon
Foil
Hot pads
Cooling rack

FOOD FACT

The largest potato grown weighed 18 pounds and 4 ounces. You could make this recipe about 10 times with just that one potato!

CHAD

FINAL ACT

CHAD'S NUTTY APPLE CRISP

Break the "Status Quo" and show off your sweeter side by sharing this fruit crisp with the apple of your eye.

1. Turn on oven to 375°F. On cutting board, use sharp knife to cut each apple into four pieces. Cut out and throw away the cores. Cut apples into thin slices. Place apple slices in a 2-quart square baking dish.

2. Put 2 tablespoons flour and the 1 tablespoon brown sugar in a small bowl. Stir with a wooden spoon. Sprinkle flour mixture over apple slices in baking dish; toss to coat. Cover with foil. Place baking dish in oven. Bake 15 minutes.

3. While apples bake, put rolled oats, 2 tablespoons flour, and the 2 tablespoons brown sugar in a medium bowl. Stir with wooden spoon until combined. Add peanut butter and use a fork to stir until the mixture looks like coarse crumbs. Stir in peanuts.

4. Use hot pads to carefully pull out oven rack. Carefully uncover apple mixture; sprinkle with oat mixture. Use hot pads to push oven rack back in place. Bake, uncovered, 15 to 20 minutes more or until apples are tender and topping is golden brown. Turn off oven. Use hot pads to remove baking dish from oven and place on cooling rack. Let cool slightly before serving. Makes 8 servings.

Nutrition Facts per serving: 174 calories, 6 g total fat, 0 mg cholesterol, 51 mg sodium, 28 g carbohydrate, 4 g fiber, 4 g protein.

Ingredients

- 6 medium red and/or green cooking apples, peeled, if you like
- 2 tablespoons all-purpose flour
- 1 tablespoon brown sugar
- ⅔ cup quick-cooking rolled oats
- 2 tablespoons all-purpose flour
- 2 tablespoons brown sugar
- ¼ cup peanut butter
- 2 tablespoons chopped peanuts

Utensils

Measuring cups
Measuring spoons
Vegetable peeler, if you like
Cutting board
Sharp knife
2-quart square baking dish
Small bowl
Wooden spoon
Foil
Medium bowl
Fork
Hot pads
Cooling rack

DIVE IN

FOOD FACT Almost three jars of peanut butter are sold every second—that's 90 million jars a year!

Ingredients

3	eggs
2	egg yolks
2½	cups fat-free milk
⅓	cup sugar
1	teaspoon vanilla
¼	cup fat-free caramel ice cream topping
	Fresh raspberries

Utensils

Measuring cups
Measuring spoons
Large bowl
Wire whisk or rotary beater
Six 6-ounce oven-safe
   dessert dishes or custard cups
Large roasting pan
Hot pads
Table knives
2 cooling racks
Plastic wrap
6 dessert plates
Small spoon

FINAL ACT

WILDCATS

ZEKE'S PERFECT CRÈME BRÛLÉE

Straight from the baker himself, Zeke's crème brûlée recipe will earn you rave reviews.

1. Turn on oven to 300°F. Put eggs and egg yolks in a large bowl. Use wire whisk or rotary beater to beat eggs until well mixed. Add milk, sugar, and vanilla. Beat with wire whisk or rotary beater just until mixed.

2. Place six 6-ounce dessert dishes or custard cups in a large roasting pan. Use hot pads to pull out oven rack.* Carefully place roasting pan on oven rack. Carefully pour some of the egg mixture into each dish or cup. With the help of an adult, pour enough hot water into the roasting pan around the dishes or cups to reach halfway up the sides (be careful not to splash water into the custards).

3. Use hot pads to push oven rack back into place. Bake 50 to 55 minutes or until set. (To tell if custards are set, insert a table knife into the center of a custard. It should come out clean.) Turn off oven. Have an adult use hot pads to remove roasting pan from oven and place on cooling rack. Use hot pads to carefully remove dishes or cups from roasting pan. Place on another cooling rack. Let stand 1 hour. Cover each dish or cup with plastic wrap. Put in the refrigerator and chill at least 6 hours or up to 24 hours.

4. To serve, run a table knife around the edge of each dessert dish or custard cup to loosen custard. Place a dessert plate upside down over a custard. Have an adult grasp the plate and custard with both hands and turn the plate and custard over so the custard is upside down on the plate. Lift off the dish or cup. Repeat to unmold the remaining custards. Use a small spoon to drizzle the caramel topping over custards; top with raspberries. Makes 6 servings.

*Note: Be sure to have an adult help you with this recipe.

Nutrition Facts per serving: 182 calories, 4 g total fat, 178 mg cholesterol, 117 mg sodium, 28 g carbohydrate, 1 g fiber, 8 g protein.

FOOD FACT

The average American eats 256 eggs a year! Each one of those eggs has more than 6 grams of protein.

GAME DAY
RECIPES

Whether your game is basketball, baseball, golf, or scholastic decathlon, these recipes will fuel you up to "Get'cha Head in the Game" so you can play your best. Don't worry about the West High Knights or any other opponent; the *Wildcats* are behind you and

"We're All in This Together!"

FIRST QUARTER
Coach Bolton's Breakfast Burritos
Get'cha Head in the Game Bars

SECOND QUARTER
Single-Handed Salad
Three-on-Three Macaroni

HALFTIME
Sideline S'mores
What Team? Veggie Dip

THIRD QUARTER
MVP Quesadillas
Jason's Easy Enchiladas
East High Hot Dogs

FOURTH QUARTER
Cheer-for-the-Team Fruit Sundae
All-in-This-Together Fruit Toppers

THE **future** is a **BIG PLACE**

AWESOME
EATS FROM EAST HIGH

Ingredients

- 4   slices turkey bacon* or bacon
- ¼   cup chopped green sweet pepper
- ⅛   teaspoon salt
- ⅛   teaspoon ground cumin
- ⅛   teaspoon crushed red pepper
- 4   8-inch whole wheat or multigrain tortillas
- 8   eggs
- ¼   cup fat-free milk
- ¼   cup chopped tomato
- ½   cup shredded reduced-fat Monterey Jack cheese (2 ounces)
    Bottled hot pepper sauce, if you like
    Light dairy sour cream and/or purchased salsa, if you like

Utensils

Measuring cups
Measuring spoons
Cutting board
Sharp knife
Large nonstick skillet
Wooden spoon
Hot pads
Cooling rack
Colander
Medium bowl
Disposable container
Foil
Large bowl
Wire whisk or rotary beater
Spatula
Large spoon

COACH BOLTON'S BREAKFAST BURRITOS

Coach Bolton knows a balanced breakfast is a must to keep his players energized. Serving this protein-packed burrito is sure to lead your team to victory!

1. Turn on oven to 350°F. On the cutting board, use a sharp knife to cut bacon into small pieces. Put bacon and green pepper in a large nonstick skillet. Put skillet on burner. Turn burner to medium heat. Cook until bacon is crisp and green pepper is tender, stirring often with a wooden spoon. Turn off burner. Use hot pads to remove skillet from burner. Place skillet on cooling rack.

2. Place colander over a medium bowl. Spoon bacon mixture and juices into the colander and let the juices drain into the medium bowl. Spoon the bacon mixture back into the skillet. Put cooled fat in a disposable container and throw away. Add salt, cumin, and crushed red pepper to skillet. Save for Step 5.

3. Wrap tortillas in a sheet of foil. Put tortillas in oven. Bake about 10 minutes or until tortillas are warmed. Turn off oven. Use hot pads to remove tortillas from oven. Place on cooling rack. Save for Step 7.

4. While the tortillas are baking, put eggs and milk in a large bowl. Use wire whisk or rotary beater to beat until well mixed.

5. Put skillet with bacon mixture back on burner. Turn burner to medium heat. Cook and stir with wooden spoon 1 minute. Pour egg mixture over bacon mixture. Cook, without stirring, until mixture begins to set on the bottom and around the edge.

6. Use spatula to lift and fold the partially cooked egg mixture so the uncooked portion flows underneath. Continue cooking and folding 2 to 3 minutes or until mixture is cooked through, but is still glossy and moist. Turn off the burner. Use hot pads to remove skillet from burner. Place skillet on cooling rack. Stir in the tomato.

7. Spoon some of the egg mixture on each of the tortillas. Sprinkle with cheese and, if desired, drizzle with a little hot pepper sauce. Roll up tortillas. If you like, serve with sour cream and/or salsa. Makes 4 servings.

*Note: If using turkey bacon, coat the unheated skillet with nonstick cooking spray before cooking.

Nutrition Facts per serving: 358 calories, 19 g total fat, 448 mg cholesterol, 840 mg sodium, 18 g carbohydrate, 10 g fiber, 27 g protein.

EAST HIGH

BACKSTAGE PASS

Coach Bolton was a star player for the East High Wildcats basketball team when he was a student.

WILDCATS

TROY

WILDCATS

GET'CHA HEAD IN THE GAME BARS

No matter how much time is on the clock, you have time for breakfast with these grab-and-go bars. They'll fuel you up to help you focus on the game.

1. Turn on oven to 325°F. Line an 8x8x2-inch baking pan with foil. Coat foil with nonstick cooking spray. Save for Step 2.

2. Put rolled oats, flour, Grape Nuts cereal, and ginger in a large bowl. Stir with a wooden spoon until mixed. Put egg in a medium bowl. Beat with a fork or wire whisk until well mixed. Add beaten egg, applesauce, honey, brown sugar, and oil to the flour mixture. Stir with wooden spoon to mix well. Stir in fruit bits, sunflower seeds, and walnuts. Pour into the prepared pan, using a rubber scraper to scrape bowl and spread mixture evenly in baking pan.

3. Place baking pan in oven. Bake 30 to 35 minutes or until lightly browned around the edges. Turn off oven. Use hot pads to remove baking pan from oven. Place baking pan on cooling rack. Let stand until cooled. Use edges of foil to lift block from pan. Use a sharp knife to cut block into bars. Makes 12 bars.

Nutrition Facts per bar: 208 calories, 6 g total fat, 18 mg cholesterol, 48 mg sodium, 36 g carbohydrate, 2 g fiber, 4 g protein.

Ingredients

Nonstick cooking spray
1 cup quick-cooking rolled oats
½ cup all-purpose flour
½ cup Grape Nuts® cereal
½ teaspoon ground ginger
1 egg
⅓ cup unsweetened applesauce
¼ cup honey
¼ cup packed brown sugar
2 tablespoons cooking oil
1 16-ounce package mixed dried fruit bits
¼ cup shelled sunflower seeds
¼ cup chopped walnuts

The Future is a Big Place

Utensils

Measuring cups
Measuring spoons
8x8x2-inch baking pan
Foil
Large bowl
Wooden spoon
Medium bowl
Fork or wire whisk
Rubber scraper
Hot pads
Cooling rack
Sharp knife

EAST HIGH

WORK IT OUT

Practice makes perfect, so Troy spends extra time working on his basketball skills. Do some extra practice for your favorite sport or hobby. Whether it's soccer, dance, jump rope, volleyball, or anything else, the extra work will improve your performance and keep you moving.

SINGLE-HANDED SALAD

Think you're so good at basketball that you could play one-handed? Enjoy this wrapped-up salad with one hand while you shoot with the other.

1. On a cutting board, use sharp knife to cut the avocado lengthwise around the seed. Place one hand on each side of the avocado and twist in opposite directions to separate the halves. Firmly tap the seed with the blade of the sharp knife. When the blade catches in the seed, turn the knife to lift out the seed. Wrap one half of the avocado in plastic wrap and refrigerate it to use another time. Use a large spoon to loosen the other half of the avocado from the peel; lift out the avocado in one piece and discard the peel. Use the sharp knife to cut avocado into slices. Use the sharp knife to cut the cucumber into thin slices.

2. Place some of the lettuce, turkey, avocado, cucumber, and Monterey Jack cheese on each tortilla.

3. Tightly roll up each tortilla. If you like, use the sharp knife to halve each tortilla diagonally. Wrap each tightly with plastic wrap. Chill in the refrigerator for up to 6 hours. If you like, serve with salad dressing. Makes 2 servings.

Nutrition Facts per serving: 330 calories, 15 g total fat, 35 mg cholesterol, 1,061 mg sodium, 25 g carbohydrate, 5 g fiber, 25 g protein.

Ingredients

- 1 avocado
- ¼ of a cucumber
- ¾ cup torn romaine lettuce
- 4 ounces sliced cooked turkey breast from the deli
- ¼ cup shredded reduced-fat Monterey Jack cheese (1 ounce)
- 2 8-inch whole grain, whole wheat, or flour tortillas
- Thousand Island or ranch salad dressing, if you like

Utensils

Measuring cups
Cutting board
Sharp knife
Plastic wrap
Large spoon

Wildcat
Summer

FOOD FACT

Avocados are sometimes called alligator pears because of their green, lizardlike skin. Don't let the name scare you; avocados contain vitamin C, folate, potassium, and monounsaturated fat—all things that are part of a healthy diet.

THREE-ON-THREE MACARONI

A pile of pasta with three melty cheeses and your favorite veggies make the perfect dish after an intense scrimmage or practice.

1. Turn on oven to 350°F. Grease a 2-quart rectangular baking dish with nonstick cooking spray. Tear cheese slices into pieces. Save for Step 3.

2. Cook macaroni in a large saucepan following package directions. (To test macaroni for doneness, remove one piece with a wooden spoon, let it cool slightly, and bite into it. The center will be soft, not chewy.) When macaroni is cooked, turn off burner. Place colander in sink. Use hot pads to remove saucepan from burner. Carefully pour macaroni into the colander and let liquid drain into sink. Return drained macaroni to the large saucepan. Use a wooden spoon to stir in butter until melted.

3. Add milk, pepper, and salt. Stir in all cheeses and frozen vegetables. Spoon macaroni mixture into baking dish.

4. Put baking dish in oven. Bake, uncovered, 15 minutes. Use hot pads to pull out oven rack. Use wooden spoon to carefully stir mixture. Using hot pads, carefully push the oven rack back into place. Bake about 10 minutes more or just until mixture is heated through. (Don't overheat or it will curdle.) Turn off oven. Use hot pads to remove baking dish from oven. Place baking dish on cooling rack. Let stand 10 minutes before serving. Makes 5 servings.

Nutrition Facts per serving: 356 calories, 13 g total fat, 49 mg cholesterol, 838 mg sodium, 29 g carbohydrate, 3 g fiber, 28 g protein.

Ingredients

Nonstick cooking spray
6 slices low-fat process American cheese product (¾ ounce each)
1¾ cup dried multigrain elbow macaroni (6 ounces)
2 tablespoons butter
1 cup fat-free milk
¼ teaspoon black pepper
⅛ teaspoon salt
1½ cups shredded reduced-fat sharp cheddar cheese (6 ounces)
1 cup shredded part-skim mozzarella cheese (4 ounces)
1 cup loose-pack frozen broccoli, peas, cauliflower, or other frozen vegetables

Utensils

Measuring cups
Measuring spoons
2-quart rectangular baking dish
Large saucepan
Wooden spoon
Colander
Hot pads
Cooling rack

WILDCATS

WORK IT OUT To have enough energy to play a whole game of basketball, you need to build up your endurance. Try running, dancing, riding a bike, or playing soccer to keep you going strong.

Gabriella

WILDCATS

WILDCATS

SIDELINE S'MORES

The Wildcats basketball team needs crowd support to lead them to victory! Get everyone on the sidelines cheering with these gooey treats.

1. Put graham cracker squares on cutting board. Use a table knife to spread four of the graham cracker squares with chocolate-hazelnut spread. Spread the remaining four graham cracker squares with marshmallow creme. Place graham crackers, marshmallow sides down, on top of the squares with chocolate-hazelnut spread. Place s'mores on a microwave-safe plate.

2. Microwave, uncovered, on 100% power (high) 30 seconds.* Serve at once. Makes 4 s'mores.

Nutrition Facts per s'more: 129 calories, 4 g total fat, 0 mg cholesterol, 46 mg sodium, 21 g carbohydrate, 0 g fiber, 1 g protein.

PEANUT BUTTER S'MORES
Make as above, except use chocolate graham cracker squares and substitute peanut butter for the chocolate-hazelnut spread.

Nutrition Facts per s'more: 141 calories, 7 g total fat, 0 mg cholesterol, 95 mg sodium, 16 g carbohydrate, 1 g fiber, 4 g protein.

*Note: If you want to heat one s'more at a time, microwave on 100% power (high) 10 seconds. For two s'mores, microwave 20 seconds.

Ingredients

8 chocolate or regular graham cracker squares

3 tablespoons chocolate-hazelnut spread

3 tablespoons marshmallow creme

Utensils

Measuring spoons
Cutting board
Table knives
Microwave-safe plate

WORK IT OUT

Instead of driving to the game, walk, skate, or bike with a friend. That way, even if you're not playing in the game, you get a workout too.

WHAT TEAM? VEGGIE DIP

Not playing in the big game? Dunk from the stands with this snack and your choice of dippers. It's more brain food than junk food—perfect for the Scholastic Decathlon captain.

1. Put sour cream, cream cheese, and milk in medium bowl. Beat with an electric mixer on medium speed until smooth.

2. Stir in sweet pepper, zucchini, carrot, and chives. Season to taste with salt and black pepper. Serve immediately with cut-up vegetables, crackers, and/or tortilla chips.*
Makes 16 (2-tablespoon) servings dip.

Nutrition Facts per 2 tablespoons dip: 39 calories, 3 g total fat, 10 mg cholesterol, 57 mg sodium, 1 g carbohydrate, 0 g fiber, 2 g protein.

ITALIAN VEGGIE DIP

Make as above, except omit the sweet pepper, carrot, and chives. Stir in ¼ cup seeded and finely chopped tomato and ½ teaspoon bottled minced garlic. Stir in 1 tablespoon snipped fresh basil, oregano, and/or thyme or 1 teaspoon dried Italian seasoning, crushed. Makes 16 (2-tablespoon) servings dip.

Nutrition Facts per 2 tablespoons dip: 38 calories, 3 g fat, 10 mg cholesterol, 56 mg sodium, 1 g carbohydrate, 0 g fiber, 2 g protein.

*Note: If you like, you can cover the dip with plastic wrap and chill in the refrigerator for up to 3 days. Remove plastic wrap and stir with a spoon before serving with cut-up vegetables, crackers, and/or tortilla chips.

Ingredients

1   8-ounce carton light dairy sour cream

½   of an 8-ounce package reduced-fat cream cheese (Neufchâtel)

1   tablespoon milk

¼   cup finely chopped red or yellow sweet pepper

¼   cup finely chopped zucchini

2   tablespoons shredded carrot

1   tablespoon snipped fresh chives or green onion tops

     Salt

     Black pepper

     Cut-up vegetables, assorted crackers, and/or baked tortilla chips

Utensils

Measuring cups
Measuring spoons
Cutting board
Sharp knife
Shredder
Kitchen scissors
Medium bowl
Electric mixer
Large spoon

BACKSTAGE PASS Taylor helps stall the scholastic decathlon competition against the West High Knights by creating a chemical reaction that forces everyone to evacuate the room.

WILDCATS

EAST HIGH

The Future is a Big Place

MVP QUESADILLAS

Troy may have earned the title of MVP on the basketball team, but with this fresh quesadilla you'll be MVP of the kitchen!

1. Use a table knife to spread each of the tortillas with some of the marmalade.

2. Put some of the spinach on half of each tortilla. Top spinach with chicken strips, mango slices, and Monterey Jack cheese. Fold each tortilla over filling, pressing lightly.

3. Place a griddle or large skillet on burner. Turn burner to medium heat and let griddle or skillet get hot. (To check if the griddle or skillet is ready, carefully sprinkle a few drops of water on the surface. The water will dance across the surface when the griddle is hot enough.) Use a pancake turner to put two of the quesadillas on the griddle or into the skillet. Cook 2 to 3 minutes or until bottom is lightly browned. Use pancake turner to turn quesadillas. Cook 2 to 3 minutes more or until tortillas are browned and cheese melts. Turn off burner. Use hot pads to remove griddle or skillet from burner and place on a cooling rack. Use pancake turner to remove quesadillas from griddle or skillet. Place each quesadilla on a dinner plate.

4. Use a sharp knife to cut each quesadilla in half to serve. Makes 4 servings.

Nutrition Facts per serving: 348 calories, 11 g total fat, 50 mg cholesterol, 1,108 mg sodium, 40 g carbohydrate, 6 g fiber, 24 g protein.

Ingredients

4   7-inch multigrain flour tortillas
⅓   cup low-sugar orange marmalade
2   cups fresh baby spinach
1   6-ounce package refrigerated grilled chicken breast strips
1   cup chopped drained refrigerated mango slices
1   cup shredded reduced-fat Monterey Jack cheese (4 ounces)

Utensils

Measuring cups
Table knife
Griddle or large skillet
Pancake turner
Hot pads
Cooling rack
4 dinner plates
Sharp knife

DIVE IN

TROY

Ingredients

1	7½-ounce package frozen diced cooked chicken
	Nonstick cooking spray
8	7- or 8-inch whole wheat or multigrain flour tortillas
1	15- to 16-ounce can pinto beans or black beans, drained and rinsed
1	cup shredded reduced-fat Monterey Jack cheese (4 ounces)
1	8-ounce can no-salt-added tomato sauce
1	cup purchased salsa

Utensils

Measuring cups
3-quart rectangular baking dish
Foil
Hot pads
Cooling rack
Can opener
Colander
Medium bowl
Wooden spoons
Small bowl
Large spoon

JASON'S EASY ENCHILADAS

Make Jason's favorite dish part of your starting lineup of recipes.
After all, an easy entrée is key to a winning meal.

1. Thaw chicken following the directions on the package. Save for Step 3. Turn on oven to 350°F. Lightly coat a 3-quart rectangular baking dish with nonstick cooking spray. Save for Step 4.

2. Wrap tortillas in a sheet of foil. Put tortillas in oven. Bake about 10 minutes or until tortillas are warmed. Use hot pads to remove tortillas from oven. Place on cooling rack.

3. While tortillas are baking, put beans in a medium bowl. Use a wooden spoon to stir in chicken and ½ cup of the cheese. Put the tomato sauce in a small bowl. Use wooden spoon to stir in salsa. Stir half of the tomato sauce mixture into the chicken mixture. Save the remaining tomato sauce mixture for Step 4.

4. Spoon some of the chicken mixture on each of the warm tortillas. Roll up each tortilla. Place tortilla rolls, seam sides down, in prepared baking dish. Spoon the remaining tomato sauce mixture down the center of the filled tortillas.

5. Cover baking dish with foil. Put baking dish in oven. Bake about 30 minutes or until heated through. Use hot pads to pull out oven rack. Carefully remove foil. Sprinkle with the remaining ½ cup cheese. Using hot pads, carefully push the oven rack back into place. Bake, uncovered, about 5 minutes more or until cheese is melted. Turn off the oven. Use hot pads to remove baking dish from oven. Place baking dish on a cooling rack. Makes 8 servings.

Nutrition Facts per serving: 297 calories, 9 g total fat, 18 mg cholesterol, 954 mg sodium, 34 g carbohydrate, 15 g fiber, 20 g protein.

FOOD FACT

Pinto beans are one of the official state vegetables of New Mexico, the home state of East High School.

BEST-SHOT BLT DOGS

1. Turn on oven to 350°F. On a cutting board, use a sharp knife to cut tomato into small pieces. Put tomato in a small bowl. Save until Step 3.

2. Use a sharp knife to cut each bacon slice in half lengthwise. Wrap a piece of the bacon around each hot dog, wrapping in a spiral. Use wooden toothpicks to hold bacon in place. Put bacon-wrapped hot dogs on a baking sheet. Put baking sheet in oven. Bake about 10 minutes or until hot dogs and bacon are heated through. Turn off oven. Use hot pads to remove baking sheet from oven. Place baking sheet on cooling rack.

3. To serve, place some of the lettuce in each hot dog bun. Drizzle with the ranch dressing. Carefully remove wooden toothpicks from hot dogs and throw picks away. Put a hot dog in each bun. Top with the tomato. Makes 4 servings.

Nutrition Facts per serving: 304 calories, 7 g total fat, 27 mg cholesterol, 1,109 mg sodium, 46 g carbohydrate, 3 g fiber, 14 g protein.

Ingredients

1   tomato
2   slices fully cooked turkey bacon
4   fat-free or regular hot dogs
2   cups shredded lettuce
4   whole wheat hot dog buns (buy split buns)
¼   cup bottled reduced-calorie ranch salad dressing

Utensils

Cutting board
Sharp knife
Small bowl
Wooden toothpicks
Baking sheet
Hot pads
Cooling rack

EAST HIGH HOT DOGS

You know the Wildcats are the basketball champs, but which of these recipes will be top dog?

VICTORY CHILI DOGS

1. Put a skillet or grill pan on a burner.* Turn burner to medium heat. Put hot dogs in skillet or grill pan. Cook 5 to 6 minutes or until heated through, using tongs to turn hot dogs occasionally.

2. Use the tongs to remove hot dogs. Put a hot dog in each bun. Turn off burner and remove grill pan.

3. While the hot dogs cook, put the chili and salsa in a medium saucepan. Stir together with a wooden spoon. Put saucepan on burner. Turn burner to medium heat. Cook until heated through, stirring with wooden spoon. Turn off burner. Use hot pads to remove saucepan from burner and place on cooling rack.

4. Spoon chili mixture into a serving bowl. Put cheddar cheese and crushed chips in separate serving bowls. Serve green onions, chili, cheese, and chips with hot dogs. Makes 8 servings.

*Note: To broil, set the oven rack 4 inches from broiler. Turn on broiler. Put hot dogs on broiler pan. Put pan under broiler. Broil 3 minutes. Use hot pads to carefully pull out pan. Use tongs to turn hot dogs. Use hot pads to carefully push in pan. Broil 2 to 3 minutes more or until hot dogs are heated through. Turn off broiler. Use hot pads to remove broiler pan from oven. Place on cooling rack.

Nutrition Facts per serving: 345 calories, 7 g total fat, 26 mg cholesterol, 1,193 mg sodium, 50 g carbohydrate, 2 g fiber, 17 g protein.

Ingredients

8   fat-free or regular hot dogs
8   whole wheat hot dog buns (buy split buns)
1   15-ounce can chili without beans
½   cup purchased salsa
½   cup shredded reduced-fat cheddar cheese (2 ounces)
1   cup baked corn chips, coarsely crushed
2   green onions, sliced

Utensils

Measuring cups
Cutting board
Sharp knife
4 serving bowls
Skillet or grill pan
Tongs

Serving tray
Can opener
Medium saucepan
Wooden spoon
Hot pads
Cooling rack

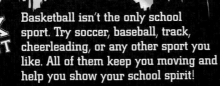

WORK IT OUT Basketball isn't the only school sport. Try soccer, baseball, track, cheerleading, or any other sport you like. All of them keep you moving and help you show your school spirit!

RYAN

48

CHEER-FOR-THE-TEAM FRUIT SUNDAE

When the game is down to the wire, the Wildcats need everyone cheering. This sundae is sure to get people on their feet.

1. Put pudding mix in medium bowl. Add milk. Use a wire whisk or rotary beater to beat the pudding mix and milk about 2 minutes or until well mixed. Cover with plastic wrap. Put in the refrigerator. Chill until the pudding is starting to set (about 10 minutes).

2. Spoon fruit into ice cream cones. Spoon the pudding over fruit. Serve immediately. Makes 4 servings.

Nutrition Facts per serving: 143 calories, 1 g total fat, 2 mg cholesterol, 406 mg sodium, 29 g carbohydrate, 2 g fiber, 4 g protein.

Ingredients

- 1 4-serving-size package sugar-free instant lemon, vanilla, or white chocolate pudding mix
- 1⅓ cups fat-free milk
- 1 cup fresh fruit (such as blueberries, sliced kiwi fruit, sliced strawberries, raspberries, or sliced bananas)
- 4 waffle ice cream cones or large waffle ice cream bowls

Utensils

Measuring cups
Medium bowl
Wire whisk or rotary beater
Plastic wrap
Large spoons

STAR

QUEEN of Lava Springs

Sharpay

WORK IT OUT

Sharpay is very competitive and she often drags Ryan into her contests. If you're feeling competitive, set up an obstacle course and challenge your friends to see who can make it through the fastest.

Dive in

WILDCATS

EAST HIGH

FOURTH QUARTER

ALL-IN-THIS-TOGETHER FRUIT TOPPERS

Celebrate a Scholastic Decathlon or basketball victory with your favorite dessert topped off with one of these fruit toppers. Pineapple or berries? The decision is yours, playmaker.

1. Put orange peel, orange juice, cornstarch, and ginger in a small bowl. Stir with a wooden spoon until cornstarch is completely mixed in. Pour into a large skillet. Add undrained pineapple to orange juice mixture; stir with wooden spoon.

2. Put skillet on burner. Turn burner to medium heat. Cook until slightly thickened and bubbly, stirring all the time with a wooden spoon. Cook and stir for 2 minutes more. Turn off burner. Use hot pads to remove skillet from heat. Place skillet on cooling rack.

3. Serve topper warm or if you like, cool to room temperature. Spoon topper over ice cream, cake slices, brownies, or yogurt. Makes 1½ cups (six ¼-cup servings).

Nutrition Facts per ¼ cup topping with ½ cup ice cream: 165 calories, 4 g total fat, 10 mg cholesterol, 46 mg sodium, 32 g carbohydrate, 1 g fiber, 4 g protein.

MIXED BERRY TOPPER

Make as above, except use 2 cups frozen mixed berries instead of the pineapple. Sprinkle each serving with chopped toasted almonds.

Nutrition Facts per ¼ cup topping with ½ cup ice cream: 152 calories, 5 g total fat, 10 mg cholesterol, 45 mg sodium, 24 g carbohydrate, 2 g fiber, 4 g protein.

Ingredients

½ teaspoon finely shredded orange peel

¼ cup orange juice

2 teaspoons cornstarch

½ teaspoon ground ginger

1 20-ounce can crushed pineapple (juice pack), undrained

Scoops of light vanilla ice cream, cake slices, brownies, or bowls of yogurt

Utensils

Measuring cups
Measuring spoons
Fine shredder
Small bowl
Wooden spoon
Large skillet
Can opener
Hot pads
Cooling rack
Ice cream scoop
Large spoon

The Future is a Big Place

WILDCATS

FOOD FACT

While many fruits grow in 3 to 4 months, a pineapple takes about 18 months to grow. A single pineapple can weigh up to 10 pounds!

SUMMER SPLASH

RECIPES

What time is it? **SUMMERTIME!** Or at least you can make it feel like summer vacation with these recipes inspired by the Wildcats' summer at Lava Springs. You'll find the perfect dish for any meal, whether you are chillin' out at the country club, just finishing a scrimmage with the U of A, or are taking a break from your lifeguard duties.

So what are you waiting for? **Dive in!**

AWESOME
EATS FROM EAST HIGH

LOST IN MUSIC

Ingredients

1	cup all-purpose flour
½	cup whole wheat flour
2	tablespoons sugar
1	tablespoon baking powder
¼	teaspoon salt
1	6-ounce container plain low-fat yogurt
½	cup orange juice
⅓	cup fat-free milk
2	eggs
1	tablespoon canola oil
1	teaspoon vanilla
1	cup fresh blueberries
	Maple syrup

Utensils

Measuring cups
Measuring spoons
Large bowl
Wooden spoon
Medium bowl
Wire whisk
Very large nonstick skillet or nonstick griddle
Pancake turner
Large baking sheet
Hot pads
2 cooling racks
6 dinner plates

RISE & SHINE

KELSI'S BERRY PANCAKES

Facing a full day as Ryan and Sharpay's rehearsal pianist is enough to keep Kelsi in bed all day. Pancakes for breakfast will always get her—and you—jumping out of the covers.

1. Turn on oven to 250°F. Put all-purpose flour, whole wheat flour, sugar, baking powder, and salt in a large bowl. Stir together with a wooden spoon. Put the yogurt, orange juice, milk, eggs, oil, and vanilla in a medium bowl; use a wire whisk to beat until smooth. Add the yogurt mixture to the flour mixture and stir with wooden spoon until a smooth batter forms.

2. Put the skillet or griddle on a burner. Turn burner to medium heat and let skillet or griddle get hot. (To check if the skillet or griddle is ready, carefully sprinkle a few drops of water on the surface. The water will dance across the surface when the skillet or griddle is hot enough.)

3. For each pancake, pour about ¼ cup of the batter onto the hot skillet or griddle. Sprinkle about 1 tablespoon of the blueberries (5 or 6 blueberries) onto each pancake. Cook over medium heat until pancakes have slightly bubbly surfaces and the edges are slightly dry. (This will take about 2 minutes.)

4. Turn pancakes over with the pancake turner. Cook until bottoms are golden brown (1 to 2 minutes more). Remove pancakes from skillet or griddle and put on a large baking sheet. Put baking sheet in the oven to keep pancakes warm.

5. Repeat until all the batter is used. Turn off burner. Use hot pads to remove skillet or griddle from the burner and place on cooling rack. Turn off oven. Use hot pads to remove baking sheet from the oven and place on cooling rack. Use pancake turner to put pancakes on plates. Serve with maple syrup. Makes 6 servings (2 pancakes per serving).

Nutrition Facts per serving: 322 calories, 5 g total fat, 72 mg cholesterol, 271 mg sodium, 63 g carbohydrate, 2 g fiber, 8 g protein.

you are the MUSIC in ME

BACKSTAGE PASS

Before Kelsi finds out she'll be a rehearsal pianist for the summer, she tells Taylor and Gabriella that her summer plans are to grow and write music.

CHAD

TROY

BET ON IT BREAKFAST TACOS

For a breakfast you can count on to prepare you for a day full of caddying, teaching kids' golf classes, or any other job, this meal is a sure thing.

1. Turn on oven to 350°F. Wrap tortillas in a sheet of foil. Put tortillas in oven. Bake about 10 minutes or until tortillas are warmed. Turn off oven. Use hot pads to remove tortilla stack from oven and place on cooling rack. Save for Step 3.

2. To make filling, lightly coat a small nonstick skillet with nonstick cooking spray. Place skillet on burner. Turn the burner to medium-high heat. Add celery and green pepper. Cook celery and green pepper until tender, stirring now and then with a wooden spoon. Stir in ham and pineapple. Cook until heated through, stirring all the time. Turn off burner. Use hot pads to remove skillet from burner and place on cooling rack. Stir in cheese.

3. Spoon about ¼ cup of the filling in the center of each warmed tortilla. Roll up tortillas. Makes 6 servings.

Nutrition Facts per serving: 250 calories, 10 g total fat, 28 mg cholesterol, 753 mg sodium, 22 g carbohydrate, 11 g fiber, 17 g protein.

SAUSAGE AND PEAR TACOS

Prepare as above, except replace celery with 2 green onions, thinly sliced; replace ham with one 7-ounce package (10 links) light brown-and-serve sausage links, thawed if frozen and cut into 1-inch pieces; and replace crushed pineapple with two 4-ounce individual-serving-size containers diced pears in light syrup, drained.

Nutrition Facts per serving: 274 calories, 13 g total fat, 27 mg cholesterol, 720 mg sodium, 23 g carbohydrate, 11 g fiber, 18 g protein.

Ingredients

6   8-inch whole wheat or plain flour tortillas
     Nonstick cooking spray
⅓   cup chopped celery
⅓   cup chopped green sweet pepper
1   cup chopped cooked ham
1   8-ounce can crushed pineapple (juice pack) drained or ¾ cup finely chopped apple
1   cup shredded reduced-fat cheddar cheese (4 ounces)

Utensils

Measuring cups
Foil
Hot pads
Cooling rack
Small nonstick skillet
Colander
Can opener
Wooden spoon

EAST HIGH

WILDCATS

FOOD FACT

Making one pound of cheese requires about 10 pounds of milk from a dairy cow.

TAYLOR

LUNCH AT LAVA SPRINGS

TAYLOR'S TROPICAL STIR-FRY

Taylor's worked hard all summer long at Lava Springs, but she could still have fun in the sun with this tasty dish. Try it yourself for a taste of the tropics.

Ingredients

- 1 tablespoon canola oil
- 12 ounces packaged skinless, boneless chicken breast stir-fry strips, cut into bite-size pieces, if you like
- 1 16-ounce package frozen stir-fry vegetables (any combination you like)
- 2 3-ounce packages ramen noodles
- 1 8-ounce can pineapple chunks (juice pack)
- ½ cup bottled stir-fry sauce
- ⅓ cup water

Utensils

Measuring cups
Measuring spoons
Medium skillet with lid
Cutting board, if needed
Sharp knife, if needed
Wooden spoon
Medium bowl
Can opener
Hot pads
Cooling rack

1. Put oil into medium skillet. Put the skillet on a burner. Turn burner to medium-high heat and let skillet get hot. (To check if the skillet is ready, carefully sprinkle a few drops of water on the surface. The water will dance across the surface when the skillet is hot enough.) Add chicken to skillet; cook about 6 minutes or until chicken pieces are no longer pink, stirring chicken all the time with wooden spoon. Add frozen vegetables to the skillet. Cover skillet with the lid. Cook 5 to 7 minutes or until vegetables are tender but still slightly crunchy.

2. While vegetables are cooking, open the noodles. Break each block into small pieces and put in a medium bowl. Throw away the seasoning packets.

3. Add pineapple chunks and juice, noodles, stir-fry sauce, and the water to the vegetables and chicken in the skillet. Use the wooden spoon to stir until the liquid covers all of the pieces.

4. Bring mixture to boiling; turn heat to medium-low. Cover skillet with lid and cook about 3 minutes or until noodles are tender, stirring now and then with wooden spoon. Turn off burner. Use hot pads to remove skillet from burner and place on cooling rack. Makes 4 servings.

Nutrition Facts per serving: 424 calories, 12 g total fat, 49 mg cholesterol, 1,233 mg sodium, 49 g carbohydrate, 3 g fiber, 27 g protein.

BACKSTAGE PASS

Taylor is the first Wildcat to find out that Mr. Fulton banned the Lava Springs staff from participating in the talent show.

LUNCH AT LAVA SPRINGS

LAVA SPRINGS CLUB SANDWICH

As VIP members, Ryan and Sharpay run the show at Lava Springs. Their kitchen staff could whip up one of these sandwiches with the snap of their fingers—and you can too.

1. For mustard sauce, put mayonnaise dressing, mustard, honey, milk, and pepper in a small bowl; stir with wooden spoon until mixed. Save for Step 2.

2. On the bottom half of each roll, layer some of the turkey, ham, lettuce, and tomato. Drizzle with the mustard sauce. Add top halves of rolls. If you like, serve with pickle slices or spears. Makes 6 sandwiches.

Nutrition Facts per sandwich: 199 calories, 6 g total fat, 37 mg cholesterol, 1,042 mg sodium, 20 g carbohydrate, 3 g fiber, 17 g protein.

Ingredients

¼   cup light mayonnaise dressing or salad dressing

1½ teaspoons yellow mustard

1½ teaspoons honey

1½ teaspoons milk

⅛   teaspoon black pepper

6   whole wheat dinner rolls (each about 3 inches in diameter) (buy split rolls)

8   ounces thinly sliced cooked turkey or lean pork roast

8   ounces thinly sliced cooked ham

1   cup shredded lettuce

6   large tomato slices

6   dill pickle slices or spears, if you like

Utensils

Measuring cups
Measuring spoons
Small bowl
Wooden spoon

RYAN

Sharpay

QUEEN of Lava Springs

WORK IT OUT During the summer, playing golf keeps the Evans family moving. Give golf a try (without the golf cart of course). Even if you never hit the ball, all the walking is good for you.

Ingredients

- ¾ cup fat-free or low-fat dairy sour cream
- ¾ cup frozen light whipped dessert topping, thawed
- 1 teaspoon vanilla
- ⅛ teaspoon ground cinnamon
- 3 8-inch plain or whole wheat flour tortillas
- Nonstick cooking spray
- 2 teaspoons sugar
- ⅛ teaspoon ground cinnamon
- 3 cups fresh raspberries and/or blackberries
- 2 tablespoons sliced almonds, toasted*
- 1 tablespoon grated semisweet chocolate

Utensils

Measuring cups
Measuring spoons
Grater
2 small bowls
Wooden spoon
Plastic wrap
Small spoon
Cutting board
Sharp knife
2 baking sheets
Hot pads
2 cooling racks
6 dessert plates

you are the MUSIC in ME

MAKE-A-SPLASH
BERRY NACHOS

As a Lava Springs lifeguard, Gabriella knows serving these sweet chips will make a huge splash at snack time.

1. Turn on oven to 400°F. Put sour cream, dessert topping, vanilla, and ⅛ teaspoon cinnamon in a small bowl. Stir with a wooden spoon to mix well. Cover bowl with plastic wrap and place in the refrigerator while preparing tortillas.

2. Coat both sides of each tortilla with nonstick cooking spray. Put sugar and ⅛ teaspoon cinnamon in a small bowl; stir with a small spoon until mixed. Sprinkle sugar mixture over both sides of each tortilla. On a cutting board, use a sharp knife to cut each tortilla into eight wedges. Place tortilla wedges in a single layer on baking sheets.

3. Place baking sheets in oven. Bake 8 to 10 minutes or until wedges are crisp. Turn off oven. Use hot pads to remove baking sheets from oven and place on cooling racks. Let stand until cool.

4. To serve, place some tortilla wedges on each dessert plate. Top tortilla wedges with fresh berries and sour cream mixture. Sprinkle with almonds and grated chocolate. Makes 6 servings.

*Note: To toast almonds, turn on oven to 350°F. Place almonds in a pie pan. Place pie pan in oven. Bake 5 minutes. Use hot pads to remove pie pan from oven. Use a wooden spoon to stir almonds. Use hot pads to return pie pan to oven. Bake about 5 minutes more or until almonds are golden brown. Turn off oven. Use hot pads to remove pie pan from oven. Place pie pan on cooling rack. Let stand until cool.

Nutrition Facts per serving: 148 calories, 4 g total fat, 3 mg cholesterol, 106 mg sodium, 25 g carbohydrate, 5 g fiber, 3 g protein.

SMILE

Gabriella

EAST HIGH

Dive In!

WORK IT OUT
Swimming is a fun way to get a great workout. From head to toe, swimming uses almost every muscle in your body.

STRAWBERRY-BANANA SMOOTHIE

1. If using kiwi fruit, use sharp knife to peel kiwi; cut peeled kiwi into slices. Save kiwi for Step 3.

2. Put banana, strawberries, and yogurt in blender container. Cover blender with lid and blend on high speed until smooth. With blender running, add ice cubes, one at a time, through the opening in the lid and blend until smooth. Turn off blender.

3. Pour into glasses. Use rubber scraper to scrape all of the drink out. If you like, top each glass with a kiwi slice. Serve at once. Makes 8 (4-ounce) servings.

Nutrition Facts per serving: 54 calories, 1 g total fat, 1 mg cholesterol, 15 mg sodium, 12 g carbohydrate, 2 g fiber, 2 g protein.

Ingredients

1   kiwi fruit, if you like
1   banana, cut up
4   cups sliced fresh strawberries
1   6-ounce carton vanilla low-fat yogurt
1   cup ice cubes

Utensils

Measuring cups
Cutting board
Table knife
Sharp knife, if needed
Blender
8 small glasses
Rubber scraper

PEACH SHAKE

1. Put peach slices, milk, honey, and vanilla in blender container.

2. Cover blender with lid and blend on high speed until mixture is smooth. Turn off blender. Pour into glasses. Use rubber scraper to get all of the drink out of the blender. Serve at once. Makes 3 (about 9-ounce) servings.

Nutrition Facts per serving: 145 calories, 3 g total fat, 11 mg cholesterol, 72 mg sodium, 25 g carbohydrate, 2 g fiber, 5 g protein.

Ingredients

2   cups frozen unsweetened peach slices
1¾ cups fat-free milk
1   tablespoon honey
1   teaspoon vanilla

Utensils

Measuring cups
Measuring spoons
Blender
3 glasses
Rubber scraper

I NEED A BREAK

FABULOUS FRUIT SMOOTHIES

With three tasty, fruity flavors to choose from, these icy drinks meet Sharpay's simple request—they are fabulous!

MANGO-PAPAYA SMOOTHIE

1. Put banana, mango, papaya, and pineapple in blender container. Add apple juice and honey. Cover blender with lid and blend on high speed until mixture is smooth.

2. With blender running, add ice cubes, one at a time, through the opening in the lid and blend until smooth. Turn off blender. Pour into glasses. Use the rubber scraper to scrape all of the drink out. Serve at once.
Makes 4 (8-ounce) servings.

Nutrition Facts per serving: 106 calories, 0 g total fat, 0 mg cholesterol, 3 mg sodium, 28 g carbohydrate, 3 g fiber, 1 g protein.

Ingredients

1   medium banana, cut up
1   cup drained, refrigerated jarred sliced mango
1   cup drained, refrigerated jarred sliced papaya
½   cup fresh pineapple cubes or canned pineapple chunks (juice pack), drained
¼   cup apple juice
1   tablespoon honey
1   cup ice cubes

Utensils

Measuring cups
Measuring spoons
Colander
Cutting board
Table knife
Blender
Rubber scraper
4 glasses

Sharpay

FOOD FACT
The largest strawberry was grown in England in 1983. It weighed 8.17 ounces, the same as a big apple!

DIVE IN

DINNER INVITATION

MEMBERS-ONLY CALZONES

To enjoy a meal like this at Lava Springs, you'd have to be a member. Make your dinner guests honorary members like Troy, so they can try these delicious stuffed pockets.

1. Turn on oven to 400°F. Line a baking sheet with foil; lightly grease foil with nonstick cooking spray. Save for Step 3. Unroll pizza dough. On a lightly floured surface, pat or use a rolling pin to roll dough into a 15x10-inch rectangle. Use sharp knife to cut dough in half crosswise, then cut in half lengthwise to make four rectangles.

2. Use a small metal spatula to spread some of the mustard over one side of each dough rectangle. Using half of the cheese, put some cheese on one half of each rectangle, cutting or tearing slices to fit. Top with ham. Top with the remaining cheese, cutting or tearing slices to fit. Using a pastry brush, brush edges of the dough rectangles with water. For each calzone, fold dough over filling to opposite edge, stretching slightly if needed to fit. Use the tines of a fork to press edges to seal.

3. Put calzones on prepared baking sheet. Use a fork to prick tops. If you like, brush tops with milk for a more golden crust.

4. Put baking sheet in oven. Bake about 15 minutes or until calzones are golden brown. Turn off oven. Use hot pads to remove baking sheet from oven and place on cooling rack. Let stand 5 minutes before serving. Makes 4 servings.

Nutrition Facts per serving: 334 calories, 12 g total fat, 53 mg cholesterol, 1,131 mg sodium, 33 g carbohydrate, 1 g fiber, 24 g protein.

Ingredients

Nonstick cooking spray
8   ounces thinly sliced cooked low-fat ham, chopped
1   13.8-ounce package refrigerated pizza dough
¼   cup Dijon-style mustard
4   ounces sliced Swiss or provolone cheese
Water
Milk, if you like

Utensils

Measuring cups
Cutting board
Sharp knife
Baking sheet
Foil
Rolling pin, if you like
Ruler
Small metal spatula
Pastry brush
Fork
Hot pads
Cooling rack

EAST HIGH
TROY

BACKSTAGE PASS While eating at Lava Springs as an honorary member, Troy turns away the food Chad serves him because Troy wanted Swiss cheese, not what Chad brought.

Ingredients

12 ounces lean ground beef

2½ cups purchased spaghetti sauce

6 dried lasagna noodles

1½ cups cottage cheese

1½ cups shredded part-skim mozzarella cheese (6 ounces)

2 tablespoons grated Parmesan cheese, if you like

Utensils

Measuring cups
Measuring spoons
Large skillet
Wooden spoon
Hot pads
Cooling rack
Colander
Medium bowl
Disposable container
2-quart rectangular baking dish
Rubber scraper
Large spoon
Foil
Tongs
Table knife
Pancake turner
8 dinner plates

DINNER INVITATION

EVENING ACTIVITY: LASAGNA DINNER

As activities coordinator, Taylor specializes in planning meals that are sure to please. Make this Italian dinner to see for yourself!

1. Turn on oven to 350°F. Put ground beef in a large skillet. Put skillet on burner. Turn burner to medium-high heat. Break up meat with a wooden spoon. Cook until no pink color is left in meat, stirring now and then with the wooden spoon. This will take about 10 minutes. Turn off burner. Use hot pads to remove skillet from burner and place skillet on cooling rack.

2. Place colander over a medium bowl. Spoon meat and juices into colander and let juices drain into the bowl. Spoon meat back into skillet. Put cooled juices in a disposable container and throw away.

3. Spoon 1 cup of the spaghetti sauce into a 2-quart rectangular baking dish and spread evenly with a rubber scraper. Stir the remaining 1½ cups spaghetti sauce into the meat in skillet.

4. Place two of the uncooked lasagna noodles on the sauce in the baking dish. Spoon one-third of the meat mixture on top of the noodles; use rubber scraper to spread meat mixture evenly. Use a large spoon to spread ¾ cup of the cottage cheese over the meat. Sprinkle ½ cup of the mozzarella cheese over cottage cheese. Layer on another two uncooked noodles, one-third of the meat mixture, the rest of the cottage cheese, and ½ cup of the mozzarella cheese. Layer the remaining uncooked noodles, meat mixture, and mozzarella cheese. (Layers will be high in the dish but will cook down.) If you like, sprinkle Parmesan cheese over the top.

5. Cover baking dish with foil. Put covered baking dish in oven. Bake 1 hour. Turn off oven. Use hot pads to remove baking dish from oven and place on cooling rack; let stand with foil cover in place 15 minutes. Using tongs, carefully remove foil from dish so steam escapes away from you. Use table knife to cut into rectangles. Use pancake turner to lift lasagna from pan and place on dinner plates. Makes 8 servings.

Nutrition Facts per serving: 245 calories, 7 g total fat, 39 mg cholesterol, 636 mg sodium, 21 g carbohydrate, 2 g fiber, 23 g protein.

WORK IT OUT

The staff baseball game was a great way for all the Wildcats to exercise as a group. Gather your own friends together for a game of baseball, kickball, dodgeball, or another favorite game.

LEMON-BLUEBERRY PARFAITS

1. In a medium bowl, make pudding mix following directions on package, except use 2 cups milk instead of the amount called for on the package. Add sour cream, finely shredded lemon peel, and lemon juice and stir with a wooden spoon until well mixed.

2. Spoon half of the pudding mixture into four parfait glasses. Top with half of the cake cubes and half of the berries. Add the remaining cake cubes. Spoon the remaining pudding mixture over the cake. Top with the remaining berries.

3. Cover parfait glasses with plastic wrap. Put in the refrigerator and chill until serving time or up to 4 hours. If you like, top each parfait with a lemon wedge. Makes 4 servings.

Nutrition Facts per serving: 150 calories, 1 g total fat, 2 mg cholesterol, 539 mg sodium, 30 g carbohydrate, 1 g fiber, 6 g protein.

Ingredients

1   4-serving-size package fat-free, sugar-free instant vanilla pudding mix
2   cups fat-free milk
¼   cup fat-free or light dairy sour cream
2   teaspoons finely shredded lemon peel
1   tablespoon lemon juice
2   cups angel food cake cubes (about 2½ ounces)
1   cup fresh blueberries or raspberries
4   lemon peel wedges, if you like

Utensils

Measuring cups
Measuring spoons
Fine shredder
Citrus juicer
Cutting board
Sharp knife
Vegetable peeler, if you like
Medium bowl
Wooden spoon
4 parfait glasses
Plastic wrap

BET on It

POP & LOCK PARFAITS

Even though hip-hop is Martha's passion, when she's in the Lava Springs kitchen, she does more chopping and slicing than popping and locking.

FRUIT SUNDAE PARFAITS

1. Chill two tall parfait glasses.

2. Use a large spoon to put ¼ cup of the frozen yogurt in the bottom of each chilled glass. Top each with 2 tablespoons of the crushed vanilla wafers and ¼ cup of the fruit. Repeat layers. Top each with another ¼ cup of the frozen yogurt. Drizzle each with 1 tablespoon of the strawberry topping, if you like.

3. If you like, spoon some of the whipped topping on each parfait and top with a cherry. Serve with long-handled spoons. Makes 2 servings.

Nutrition Facts per serving: 252 calories, 5 g total fat, 15 mg cholesterol, 153 mg sodium, 47 g carbohydrate, 2 g fiber, 5 g protein.

Ingredients

1½   cups frozen low-fat vanilla or fruit-flavor yogurt or light ice cream

½   cup coarsely crushed vanilla wafers or honey or cinnamon graham crackers

1   cup fresh fruit (such as sliced strawberries or bananas; peeled, sliced kiwi fruit, peaches, or mangoes; cut-up pineapple; raspberries; and/or blueberries)

2   tablespoons strawberry ice cream topping, if you like

¼   cup frozen light whipped dessert topping, thawed, if you like

2   maraschino cherries with stems, if you like

Utensils

Measuring cups
Measuring spoons
2 tall parfait glasses
Large spoon
2 long-handled spoons

FOOD FACT

Yogurt is a great healthful treat. It has lots of calcium, vitamins, and protein to help keep you strong and healthy so you can pop and lock as long as you want!

STAR

STAR DAZZLE AWARD-WINNING DESSERTS

CHEWY JAZZ SQUARES

With the rest of the Wildcats by his side, Ryan can create great dances and great dishes, like these jazzed-up bars.

1. Turn on oven to 350°F. Line a baking pan with foil, letting the foil hang over the ends of the pan; lightly coat foil with nonstick cooking spray. Save for Step 4.

2. Put brown sugar and butter in a medium saucepan. Place saucepan on burner. Turn burner to medium heat. Cook until butter melts and mixture is smooth, stirring now and then with a wooden spoon. Turn off burner. Use hot pads to remove saucepan from burner and place on cooling rack.

3. Stir applesauce, almond extract, and vanilla into butter mixture. Add eggs, one at a time, beating with wooden spoon after each egg is added until mixture is combined. Put all-purpose flour, whole wheat flour, and baking powder in a small bowl. Stir with wooden spoon to mix. Add flour mixture to butter mixture, stirring until combined. Stir in dried cherries.

4. Spoon batter into prepared baking pan, spreading evenly. Sprinkle with almonds. Put baking pan in oven. Bake about 25 minutes or until golden brown. Turn off oven. Use hot pads to remove baking pan from oven and place on a cooling rack. Let stand in pan until cool.

5. To serve, use foil to lift baked mixture out of pan. Use table knife to cut into bars. Makes 24 bars.

Nutrition Facts per serving: 164 calories, 7 g total fat, 31 mg cholesterol, 69 mg sodium, 25 g carbohydrate, 1 g fiber, 2 g protein.

Ingredients

	Nonstick cooking spray
1½	cups packed brown sugar
⅔	cup butter
½	cup unsweetened applesauce
1	teaspoon almond extract
1	teaspoon vanilla
2	eggs
1	cup all-purpose flour
1	cup whole wheat flour
1½	teaspoons baking powder
½	cup dried cherries
½	cup sliced almonds

Utensils

Measuring cups
Measuring spoons
13x9x2-inch baking pan
Foil
Medium saucepan
Wooden spoon
Hot pads
Cooling rack
Small bowl
Table knife

RYAN

BACKSTAGE PASS Ryan's code name is Jazz Square when communicating with Sharpay on a walkie-talkie.

SENIOR YEAR CELEBRATION

RECIPES

Join the rest of the Wildcats as they celebrate their senior year at East High. Saying goodbye isn't easy, but you can make it easier with these recipes that are perfect for graduation parties or any gathering with friends. Remember, ONCE A WILDCAT, ALWAYS A WILDCAT.

AWESOME
EATS FROM EAST HIGH

WILDCATS

DECISION TIME DIP

You can't make important decisions—like what college to attend—on an empty stomach.
Fill up first with this dip; it's always a good choice.

1. Use a spatula to spread ⅓ cup of the refried beans on each of six small serving plates. Top refried beans with sour cream, lettuce, salsa, and cheese. Serve with tortilla chips. Makes 6 servings.

Nutrition Facts per tablespoon dip:
137 calories, 6 g total fat, 18 mg cholesterol, 520 mg sodium, 13 g carbohydrate, 3 g fiber, 7 g protein.

Ingredients

1   16-ounce can fat-free refried beans
1   8-ounce carton light dairy sour cream
½   cup shredded lettuce
½   cup purchased salsa
½   cup reduced-fat shredded Mexican cheese blend (2 ounces)
    Baked tortilla chips

Utensils

Measuring cups
Can opener
Spatula
6 small serving plates

EAST HIGH

TROY

The Future is a Big Place

BACKSTAGE **PASS** Troy and Chad's basketball jerseys are both retired from East High.

77

JUST GETTING STARTED

CHAD'S FAVORITE FRIES

Whether you need some grub after playing ball at the U of A or in your driveway, these oven fries are a slam dunk!

1. Turn on oven to 400°F. Line a baking pan with parchment paper. Save for Step 2.

2. Scrub potatoes. On a cutting board, use a sharp knife to cut potatoes into ½-inch-wide wedges. Place wedges in a very large bowl. Add oil, salt, and pepper. Toss with a wooden spoon to coat wedges. Arrange in a single layer in prepared baking pan.

3. Put baking pan in the oven. Bake 10 minutes. Use hot pads to pull out oven rack. Use a pancake turner to turn over potato wedges. Sprinkle with Parmesan cheese. Use hot pads to push oven rack back into place. Bake about 15 minutes more or until potatoes are tender and browned. Turn off oven. Use hot pads to remove baking pan from oven and place on a cooling rack. Makes 6 servings.

Nutrition Facts per serving: 170 calories, 6 g total fat, 2 mg cholesterol, 260 mg sodium, 27 g carbohydrate, 3 g fiber, 4 g protein.

Ingredients

- 2 pounds potatoes (Yukon gold, sweet, and/or baking potatoes)
- 2 tablespoons olive oil or canola oil
- ½ teaspoon salt
- ¼ teaspoon black pepper
- ¼ cup finely shredded Parmesan cheese (1 ounce)

Utensils

Measuring cups
Measuring spoons
15x10x1-inch baking pan
Parchment paper
Cutting board
Sharp knife
Very large bowl
Wooden spoon
Hot pads
Pancake turner
Cooling rack

Get'cha HEAD in the GAME

FOOD FACT America was introduced to french fries in 1802 when President Thomas Jefferson served them at a White House dinner. Now the average American eats more than 16 pounds of french fries every year!

CEREAL-NUT MEDLEY

1. Put pretzel sticks, oat cereal, corn cereal, and peanuts in a large bowl. Stir with wooden spoon. Makes 12 servings.

Nutrition Facts per serving: 116 calories, 6 g total fat, 0 mg cholesterol, 186 mg sodium, 11 g carbohydrate, 1 g fiber, 4 g protein.

Ingredients

2   cups pretzel sticks

1   cup reduced-sugar fruit-flavor round toasted oat cereal

1   cup reduced-sugar chocolate-flavor puffed corn cereal

1   cup peanuts or sliced almonds

Utensils

Measuring cups
Large bowl
Wooden spoon

MIXIN' IT UP

These mixes don't "Stick to the Status Quo." Just like Jimmie and Donny on the basketball court, they change things up.

TACO MUNCH

1. Turn on oven to 300°F. Put cereal, crackers, pretzels, and pecans in a shallow roasting pan. Stir with a wooden spoon to mix. Save for Step 2.

2. Add chili powder and garlic powder to melted butter and stir with wooden spoon to mix. Drizzle butter mixture over cereal mixture; gently stir with wooden spoon until coated.

3. Place roasting pan in oven. Bake 10 minutes. Use hot pads to pull out oven rack. Use wooden spoon to stir cereal mixture. Use hot pads to push oven rack back into place. Bake about 10 minutes more or until lightly browned. Turn off oven. Use hot pads to remove roasting pan from oven and place on cooling rack. Add dried corn or sweet peppers and stir with wooden spoon. Spread mixture on a large piece of foil. Let stand until cool.

4. Place cooled cereal mixture in an airtight storage container. Cover with lid and seal. Store at room temperature up to 1 week. Makes 4½ cups.

Nutrition Facts per ½ cup: 145 calories, 8 g total fat, 9 mg cholesterol, 184 mg sodium, 16 g carbohydrate, 1 g fiber, 4 g protein.

Ingredients

3 cups bite-size rice square cereal or corn square cereal

2 cups small cheese-flavor fish-shape crackers

2 cups small pretzels

1 cup coarsely chopped pecans or sliced almonds

½ to 1 teaspoon chili powder

¼ teaspoon garlic powder

¼ cup butter or margarine, melted

1 cup dried corn and/or dried sweet peppers

Utensils

Measuring cups
Measuring spoons
Shallow roasting pan
Wooden spoon
Small microwave-safe bowl
Hot pads
Cooling rack
Foil
Airtight storage container

BACKSTAGE **PASS** The Wildcats win their second championship in a row, thanks to Jimmie's game-winning shot.

SHIRLEY TEMPLES

1. Place a strainer over a small bowl. Pour cherries into strainer. Save juice for Step 2. Save eight cherries for Step 3. Put the remaining cherries in the refrigerator to use for something else.

2. Fill glasses with ice. Add 2 tablespoons of cherry juice to each glass. Slowly pour ginger ale into glasses, pouring an equal amount into all glasses.

3. Top each glass with an orange slice and two cherries. Makes 4 (9-ounce) servings.

Nutrition Facts per serving: 204 calories, 0 g total fat, 0 mg cholesterol, 35 mg sodium, 54 g carbohydrate, 0 g fiber, 0 g protein.

Ingredients

1   10-ounce jar maraschino cherries with stems

Ice cubes

1   32-ounce bottle ginger ale or lemon-lime carbonated beverage, chilled

4   orange slices

Utensils

Measuring spoons	Strainer
Sharp knife	Small bowl
Cutting board	4 glasses

FRUITY FIZZ

1. Put both frozen juice concentrates and the water into a large pitcher or bowl. Stir with a wooden spoon until juice concentrates are dissolved. Add pineapple juice, sugar, and lime juice; stir until sugar is dissolved. Cover pitcher or bowl with plastic wrap. Place in the refrigerator and chill until serving.

2. To serve, place ice in a large punch bowl. Pour juice mixture over ice. Slowly pour in ginger ale and carbonated water, stirring gently with a wooden spoon to mix. Use a ladle to pour punch into cups. Makes 22 (8-ounce) servings.

Nutrition Facts per serving: 204 calories, 0 g total fat, 0 mg cholesterol, 35 mg sodium, 54 g carbohydrate, 0 g fiber, 0 g protein.

Ingredients

½   of a 16-ounce can (1 cup) frozen orange juice concentrate

½   of a 12-ounce can (¾ cup) frozen lemonade concentrate

4   cups water

1   46-ounce can unsweetened pineapple juice

1¼   cups sugar

2   tablespoons lime juice

Ice ring or ice cubes

2   28-ounce bottles ginger ale, chilled

1   28-ounce bottle carbonated water, chilled

Utensils

Measuring cups	Plastic wrap
Measuring spoons	Large punch bowl
Can opener	Ladle
Large pitcher or bowl	Punch cups
Wooden spoon	

JUST GETTING STARTED

CHEERS TO THE GRADUATES

Use these sparkling sippers to propose a toast to the new college kids as they say goodbye to East High.

FULL-OF-FRUIT SIPPER

1. Pour orange juice, white grape juice, and cranberry juice into a large bowl or pitcher. Stir with a wooden spoon until well mixed.

2. Slowly add the lemon-lime beverage, stirring gently. Fill each glass about two-thirds full with ice. Add fruit to glasses. Ladle or pour juice mixture into glasses. Add fresh mint to glasses, if you like.
Makes 10 (about 6-ounce) servings.

Nutrition Facts per serving: 61 calories, 0 g total fat, 0 mg cholesterol, 25 mg sodium, 15 g carbohydrate, 1 g fiber, 1 g protein.

Ingredients

- 2 cups orange juice, chilled
- 1 cup unsweetened white grape juice, chilled
- 1 cup light cranberry juice, chilled
- 1 1-liter bottle low-calorie lemon-lime carbonated beverage, chilled
  Ice cubes
- 2 cups assorted fresh fruit (such as oranges, cut into wedges; thinly sliced and halved lemons and/or limes; pineapple wedges; seedless red or green grapes; sliced, peeled, and pitted peaches; and halved strawberries)
- 6 fresh mint sprigs, if you like

Utensils

Measuring cups
Large bowl or pitcher
Wooden spoon
6 glasses
Ladle, if needed

Food Fact

Ginger ale was introduced in Ireland in 1851. The first cola beverage followed about 30 years later.

83

HEAD OF THE CLASS

GETTING-THE-PART PIZZA

Whether you prefer a performance by Sharpay or one by Tiara, everyone can agree that this pizza should be the star of your table.

1. Thaw bread dough following directions on package. Turn on oven to 375°F. Lightly coat pizza pan with nonstick cooking spray. Save for Step 2.

2. On a lightly floured surface, use a rolling pin to roll bread dough to a 12½-inch circle. Transfer dough circle to prepared pizza pan; using your fingers, pinch edge to form a rim. Prick the dough several times with a fork.

3. Place pizza pan in oven. Bake 10 minutes. Use hot pads to remove pan from oven and place on cooling rack. Use a spatula to spread pizza sauce over hot crust. Top with Canadian-style bacon or pepperoni, pepper rings, and mushrooms. Sprinkle with cheese.

4. Use hot pads to put pizza pan back into oven. Bake 20 to 25 minutes or until cheese is melted and edge of crust is browned. Turn off oven. Use hot pads to remove pizza pan from oven and place on cooling rack. If you like, sprinkle with parsley. Use pizza cutter or kitchen scissors to cut into wedges. Makes 8 servings.

Nutrition Facts per serving: 215 calories, 5 g total fat, 13 mg cholesterol, 617 mg sodium, 30 g carbohydrate, 3 g fiber, 14 g protein.

Ingredients

- 1 16-ounce loaf frozen whole wheat bread dough
   Nonstick cooking spray
- ½ cup pizza sauce
- ½ of a 6-ounce package pizza-style Canadian-style bacon or thinly sliced cooked turkey pepperoni
- 1 red or green sweet pepper
- 1½ cups thinly sliced fresh mushrooms
- 1 cup shredded reduced-fat 4-cheese Italian cheese blend or mozzarella cheese (4 ounces)
- 2 tablespoons snipped fresh flat-leaf parsley, if you like

Utensils

Measuring cups
Measuring spoons
12-inch pizza pan
Cutting board
Sharp knife
Rolling pin
Ruler
Fork
Hot pads
Cooling rack
Spatula
Pizza cutter
Kitchen scissors

star dazzle

Sharpay

WORK IT OUT

Feeling dramatic? Round up your family or friends and act out a story as it's read aloud. The crazier the better!

Ingredients

1	medium green sweet pepper
1	medium onion
1	pound lean ground beef
1	teaspoon bottled minced garlic
1	cup chopped zucchini
1	cup chopped yellow summer squash
1	cup sliced fresh mushrooms
1	16-ounce jar salsa
1	teaspoon dried basil, crushed
6 to 8	whole wheat hamburger buns or Kaiser rolls toasted (buy split buns or rolls)

Utensils

Measuring cups
Measuring spoons
Hot pads
Cooling rack
Cutting board
Sharp knife
Large skillet with lid
Wooden spoon
Colander
Medium bowl
Disposable container

HEAD OF THE CLASS

SUPER STUDENT SLOPPY JOES

Taylor certainly isn't slacking off her senior year—she's running the prom, graduation, and yearbook committees, and MORE! But a girl's got to eat and these speedy sandwiches fit into Taylor's hectic schedule.

1. On a cutting board, use a sharp knife to cut the green pepper in half from top to bottom. Pull off the stem and throw away. Remove seeds and soft white parts and throw away. Cut pepper halves into small pieces (you should have about ¾ cup). Save for Step 3. Use the sharp knife to cut the onion into small pieces (you should have about ½ cup). Place onion, ground beef, and garlic in a large skillet. Put the skillet on a burner. Turn the burner to medium-high heat. Break up meat with the wooden spoon. Cook until no pink color is left in the meat, stirring now and then with the wooden spoon. This will take about 10 minutes. Turn off burner. Use hot pads to remove skillet from burner and place on cooling rack.

2. Place colander over medium bowl. Spoon meat mixture and juices into the colander and let the juices drain into the bowl. Spoon meat back into skillet. Put cooled juices in a disposable container and throw away.

3. Add green pepper, zucchini, yellow summer squash, and mushrooms to meat mixture in skillet. Cover skillet with lid. Put covered skillet back on burner. Turn the burner to low heat. Cook 5 to 7 minutes or until vegetables are tender, stirring now and then with wooden spoon.

4. Remove lid from skillet. Add salsa and basil to mixture in skillet and stir with wooden spoon. Turn burner to high heat. Bring mixture to boiling; turn heat down to medium. Simmer, uncovered, about 10 minutes more or until most of the liquid has evaporated, stirring now and then with wooden spoon.

5. Serve mixture in toasted buns or rolls. Makes 6 to 8 servings.

Nutrition Facts per serving: 148 calories, 4 g total fat, 3 mg cholesterol, 106 mg sodium, 25 g carbohydrate, 5 g fiber, 3 g protein.

FOOD FACT

Bell peppers are a great source of vitamin C! They contain even more vitamin C than oranges and other citrus fruits.

QUEEN of Lava Springs

Ingredients

Nonstick cooking spray
¾ cup all-purpose flour
3 tablespoons granulated sugar
¼ cup butter or margarine
1 egg
1 egg white
⅔ cup granulated sugar
2 tablespoons all-purpose flour
2 tablespoons lemon juice
1 tablespoon water
¼ teaspoon baking powder
1 teaspoon finely shredded lemon peel
Sifted powdered sugar, if you like
Shredded lemon peel, if you like

Utensils

Measuring cups
Measuring spoons
Fine shredder
Citrus juicer
8x8x2-inch baking pan
2 small bowls
Wooden spoon
Pastry blender
Electric mixer
Hot pads
Cooling rack
Sharp knife
Sifter or small sieve, if you like

Queen of Lava Springs

SWEET ENDINGS

NAME-IN-LIGHTS LEMON BARS

While Sharpay and Ryan plan to light up Broadway, you can light up the faces of everyone at your table with these brightly colored bars.

1. Turn on oven to 350°F. Lightly coat baking pan with nonstick cooking spray. To make the crust, put the ¾ cup flour and the 3 tablespoons granulated sugar in a small bowl; stir with a wooden spoon to mix well. Add butter to the flour mixture. Using a pastry blender, cut down through butter. Continue cutting butter with pastry blender until butter looks like coarse crumbs and is evenly mixed with the flour. Spoon mixture into prepared baking pan. Use your fingers to press the mixture evenly in the pan. Put the baking pan in oven. Bake 15 minutes.

2. While the crust is baking, put the egg and egg white into another small bowl. Beat with an electric mixer on medium speed until the eggs are well mixed and bubbly. Add the ⅔ cup granulated sugar, the 2 tablespoons flour, the lemon juice, the water, and baking powder to eggs. Beat with electric mixer on medium speed about 3 minutes or until slightly thickened. Add lemon peel and stir with a wooden spoon.

3. Use hot pads to remove baking pan from oven. Place baking pan on a cooling rack. Pour egg mixture over hot crust. Use hot pads to put the baking pan back in the oven.

4. Bake 20 to 25 minutes more or until edges are light brown and center is set. Turn off oven. Use hot pads to remove baking pan from oven and place on cooling rack. Let stand until cool.

5. When cool, use a sharp knife to cut the block into nine squares. Cut each square diagonally to make triangles. If you like, top with sifted powdered sugar and/or additional shredded lemon peel. Makes 18 triangles.

Nutrition Facts per triangle: 85 calories, 3 g total fat, 19 mg cholesterol, 40 mg sodium, 14 g carbohydrate, 0 g fiber, 1 g protein.

Sharpay

RYAN

WORK IT OUT

Ryan and Sharpay get a lot of exercise dancing. Follow their lead by choreographing a dance or just put on your favorite song and dance!

Ingredients

2	ounces unsweetened chocolate
2	eggs
⅔	cup granulated sugar
¼	cup canola oil
1	teaspoon baking powder
1	teaspoon vanilla
¼	teaspoon ground cinnamon
½	cup whole wheat flour
½	cup all-purpose flour
¼	cup powdered sugar

Utensils

Measuring cups
Measuring spoons
Small microwave-safe bowl
Wooden spoon
Hot pads
Large bowl
Electric mixer
Rubber scraper
Plastic wrap
2 large cookie sheets
Small shallow bowl
2 cooling racks
Pancake turner
Waxed paper, if storing
Airtight container, if storing

The Future is a Big Place

PERFECTLY PAIRED COOKIES

The flavor combination of chocolate and cinnamon make the perfect couple—just like Troy and Gabriella.

1. Place chocolate in a small microwave-safe bowl. Place bowl in the microwave oven. Microwave on 70% power (medium-high) 1 minute; stir with a wooden spoon. Microwave on 70% power (medium-high) 15 seconds; stir with a wooden spoon. Repeat another five times. (The total time in the microwave oven is 2½ minutes at 70% power.) Stir with wooden spoon until chocolate is melted and smooth. Use hot pads to remove bowl from microwave oven. Let stand until cool.

2. Place cooled melted chocolate in a large bowl. Add eggs, granulated sugar, oil, baking powder, vanilla, and cinnamon. Beat with an electric mixer on medium speed until combined. Slowly add the whole wheat flour and the all-purpose flour, continuing to beat until a soft dough forms (be sure to stop the mixer a few times and scrape down the sides of the bowl with a rubber scraper). Cover the bowl with plastic wrap. Place in the freezer 30 to 60 minutes or until the dough is easy to shape.

3. Turn on oven to 375°F. Lightly grease two large cookie sheets. Remove bowl from freezer. Using your hands, divide dough into three equal portions. Divide each portion into ten pieces (30 pieces total). Roll each piece between your hands to shape into a ball. Put powdered sugar in a small shallow bowl. Roll balls in powdered sugar until coated. Place balls 1 inch apart on prepared cookie sheets.

4. Place one cookie sheet in the oven. Bake about 8 minutes or until edges of cookies are set and tops are dry (be careful not to overbake). Use hot pads to remove cookie sheet from oven. Place cookie sheet on a cooling rack. Use pancake turner to remove cookies from cookie sheet and place on another cooling rack. Repeat to bake cookies on the remaining cookie sheet. Turn off oven. Cool cookies completely. Makes 30 cookies.

To Store: Layer baked cookies between waxed paper in an airtight container. Cover with lid and seal. Store at room temperature for up to 3 days or freeze for up to 3 months.

Nutrition Facts per serving: 66 calories, 3 g total fat, 14 mg cholesterol, 13 mg sodium, 9 g carbohydrate, 1 g fiber, 1 g protein.

FOOD FACT

Cinnamon was one of the first known spices in the world. Today it is one of the world's most popular.

SWEET ENDINGS

WILDCAT RED & WHITE BITES

Show your East High pride with these tiny tarts in the school's colors.
Remember, once a Wildcat, always a Wildcat.

1. To make the filling, put granulated sugar and cornstarch in a small saucepan. Stir with a wooden spoon to mix; stir in the cold water. Stir in frozen cherries and berries. Place saucepan on burner. Turn burner to medium heat. Cook until boiling, stirring all the time. Cook 2 minutes more, stirring all the time. Turn off burner. Use hot pads to remove saucepan from burner and place on cooling rack. Let stand until almost cool.

2. While filling is cooling, place white baking chocolate in a small microwave-safe bowl. Place in microwave oven. Microwave on 50% power (medium) 45 seconds. Use hot pads to remove bowl from microwave. Stir with a small spoon. Return to microwave. Microwave on 50% power (medium) 45 seconds to 1 minute 15 seconds more or until melted and smooth when stirred.

3. Use a small spoon to spoon filling into phyllo dough shells. Drizzle melted white chocolate over tarts. If you like, top with fresh raspberries. Makes 15 tarts.

Nutrition Facts per tart: 44 calories,
2 g total fat, 0 mg cholesterol, 12 mg sodium,
6 g carbohydrate, 0 g fiber, 1 g protein.

Ingredients

2	tablespoons granulated sugar
1½	teaspoons cornstarch
2	tablespoons cold water
⅓	cup frozen pitted tart red cherries
¼	cup frozen raspberries or blueberries
1	ounce white baking chocolate (with cocoa butter)
1	2.1-ounce package baked miniature phyllo dough shells (15)
	Fresh raspberries, if you like

Utensils

Measuring cups
Measuring spoons
Small saucepan
Wooden spoon
Hot pads
Cooling rack
Small microwave-safe bowl
2 small spoons

BACKSTAGE PASS Now that their years at East High are over, the Wildcats are headed all over the country. Troy is going to college at Berkeley, Gabriella is attending Stanford, Chad will be playing ball at the U of A, and Ryan and Sharpay are going to perform on Broadway.

93

LOST IN MUSIC

INDEX

PLAN A WILDCAT BASH!

Use your favorite recipes from this book and the tips below to host the ultimate "High School Musical" party.

INVITE

Kick things off with an awesome invitation.

Make invitations that look like items from the movies, such as the following:

- Pennants
- Basketballs
- Tickets

Be sure to include all the information you need in the invitations:

- Who or what the party is for
- Date and time of the party
- Where the party is being held
- An email address or a phone number to call or text with questions or to RSVP

DECORATE

Set the stage by transforming your party space into a scene right out of the movies!

Decorate with red and white balloons and streamers.

Hang "High School Musical" posters. If you want to make your own posters, here are some ideas:

- What team? Wildcats!
- Beat West High
- Go Wildcats!

Use "High School Musical" plates, cups, napkins, and tablecloths.

Make a red carpet out of towels, disposable tablecloths, or construction paper. Take pictures of everyone making their red carpet entrance.

PLAY

Let everyone get in on the action with fun games.

Character quotes

- Before the party, write on red or white index cards quotes from the movies and the people who said them. Have each guest take turns reading a quote and let everyone else guess which character said it.

Sing-along

- If you have a karaoke machine, set it up and let your guests perform like Troy and Gabriella when they first met at the New Year's party. If you don't have karaoke, play the "High School Musical" soundtracks and let everyone sing along!

Who am I?

- When your guests arrive, put on each person's back a nametag with the name of one of the characters from "High School Musical". Don't let them know who they are! Have the other guests give clues about who they are until they figure it out. For example, if someone is wearing a Chad nametag, you could tell him or her,"You like to play basketball, you have curly hair, and you like Taylor."

MAKE

Give everyone a chance to make a souvenir to remember your party.

Dressing Room stars

- Using construction paper, markers, glue, glitter, and stickers, design a star to hang on your bedroom door.

East High School pennants

- Using red and white felt, scissors, and glue, make your own East High pennants.

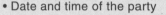